Historical Association Studies

British Politics Since 1945:
The Rise and Fall of Consensus

Historical Association Studies

General Editor: M. E. Chamberlain

The Historical Association, founded in 1906, brings together people who share an interest in, and love for, the past. It aims to further the study and teaching of history at all levels: teacher and student, amateur and professional. This is one of over 100 publications available at very preferential rates to members. Membership also includes journals at generous discounts and gives access to courses, conferences, tours and regional and local activities. Full details are available from The Secretary, The Historical Association, 59a Kennington Park Road, London SE11 4JH, telephone: 071-735 3901.

British Politics Since 1945
The Rise and Fall of Consensus

David Dutton

Basil Blackwell

First published 1991

Basil Blackwell Ltd
108 Cowley Road, Oxford, OX4 1JF, UK

Basil Blackwell, Inc.
3 Cambridge Center
Cambridge, Massachusetts 02142, USA

British Library Cataloguing in Publication Data

A CIP catalogue record for this book is available from the British Library.

Library of Congress Cataloging in Publication Data

Dutton, David, 1947–
British politics since 1945: the rise and fall of consensus/David Dutton.
 p. cm. – (Historical Association studies)
Includes bibliographical references and index.
ISBN 0–631–18097–4 (hb.) 0–631–16278–X (pbk.)
1. Great Britain – Politics and government – 1945– 2. Consensus
 (Social sciences) I. Title. II. Series.
DA589.7.D87 1991
320.941–dc20   90–43735 CIP

Typeset in 11 on 13 pt Ehrhardt
by Setrite Typesetters, Hong Kong
Printed in Great Britain Billing & Sons Ltd, Worcester

For Ted and Vera

Contents

Preface

The first damaging characteristic of our post-war politics
has been that comparatively small changes in public
opinion have led to violent switches in public policy of a
kind not experienced by the multi-party democracies of
Europe or the two-party democracy of the United States.
(Steel, 1980, p. 159)

David Steel, then leader of the Liberal Party, wrote these
words a decade ago. His purpose, it must be said, was primarily
political rather than historical. In a sympathetic analysis of the
Lib-Lab pact of 1977−8, Steel sought to encourage acceptance
of the idea that parties can and should co-operate with one
another, as systems of proportional representation oblige them
to do on the Continent. In a further condemnation of the
pattern of postwar British politics, Steel went on:

Each government devotes much of its energy to undoing
whatever its predecessor did, and nowadays the ink is not
dry on a major Parliamentary Bill before Her Majesty's
opposition is publicly pledged to repeal it. Each swing of
the political pendulum threatens to take the country on
yet more violently diverse directions to left and right.
(Steel, 1980, p. 160)

Neither comment is likely to survive the judgement of history. This short book aims to present a very different analysis of the reality of British politics after 1945, in which continuity rather than change was the order of the day. It is one which continues to have much significance for the contemporary political debate, though not in the sense that David Steel implied.

This book owes much to the scholarship of others. Some measure of this debt is indicated in the references. But to survey nearly half a century of history in such a brief span necessitates considerable compression and omission. The reader who wishes to take the subject further is urged to consult the works listed in the bibliography.

David Dutton
Liverpool, 1990

Introduction

The postwar years in British politics have now become a legitimate area of academic historical enquiry. The thirty-year rule, which determines the availability of governmental records, means that, at the time of writing, the archives of the period up to 1959 are open to scholarly inspection. The fruits of research on these archives have begun to work their way into the published academic literature on the 1940s and 1950s. The publication of detailed diaries and memoirs by leading political figures, often after a much shorter interval of time than was thought seemly a couple of generations ago, has helped to fill many of the gaps of knowledge in the period still covered by the thirty-year rule. The use of new techniques, such as the interviewing of surviving participants, together with the undoubtedly closer contemporary scrutiny to which modern government is now subjected — notwithstanding the widely expressed concern about excessive secrecy in Whitehall — have further added to the availability of evidence for the contemporary British historian. The result has been the accumulation of a by now extensive literature covering the forty-five years since the end of the Second World War.

Furthermore, the passage of those years has been sufficient to enable historians to stand back and discern a distinct pattern of development over the period as a whole. It is that pattern which this book will attempt to explore. The argument is that for about a quarter of a century after 1945 there existed in this country, despite the superficial appearance of alternating governments of differing political complexion, a broad consensus between the two leading political parties. It is argued that this consensus, which came under increasing strain in the 1960s, broke down in the following decade and that the last twenty years have been characterized by a growing polarization of policies and ideals as between Labour and Conservative parties. Finally, there are some grounds for suggesting that the events of the very recent past imply that something of a new consensus is in the process of formation.

Any attempt to impose a structure or pattern on historical events is fraught with danger. It will be seen that the picture outlined above is open to detailed criticism. The development of British politics since the Second World War has not been quite as neat as this brief description would imply. The consensus bequeathed by the War was far from complete; it never became total; important events foretelling its demise occurred as early as the 1950s; its destruction has not perhaps been as complete as some commentators have believed. Nevertheless, if critics set too high a requirement of internal consistency, they deny the validity of almost any conceptual approach to historical study.

It is, however, only right to acknowledge that some writers have denied the very existence of a postwar consensus. Their arguments merit consideration. Perhaps the most distinguished of these critics is the Labour historian, Ben Pimlott, for whom the whole idea is a 'myth'. Pimlott stresses that consensus means harmony and that it implies that its practitioners will frequently share a common purpose. Yet, he argues, the years after 1945 saw events shaped as much by dispute as by co-operation. Contemporary politicians did not feel themselves to be part of a consensus at the time, while the term 'Butskellism', so often employed to characterize the economic consensus of the 1950s, was regarded as a term of abuse, and brought credit to neither the Conservative, Butler, nor the Socialist, Gaitskell. The theory, therefore, is a later invention, for the assumption of previous harmony is a way of contrasting the gulfs perceived to exist in the Thatcherite present. Pimlott further suggests that a middle ground consensus should have been conducive to the growth of a strong centre party, but in fact the years of supposed consensus saw the political centre — the Liberal Party — at its lowest ebb. He concludes, therefore, that 'consensus' is no more than a convenient piece of jargon 'to describe a time when we were all younger, more eager or more foolish' (Pimlott, 1988, p. 141).

It is possible to challenge Pimlott's analysis. His own definition of the idea of a consensus is somewhat tendentious and does not necessarily convey the meaning most usefully attributed to the concept in its political sense. Certainly it is not meant to suggest that there was a total absence of disputes between parties during the years when the consensus is thought to have prevailed. Contemporary observers are in any case not always the best judges of the nature of the party political divide at any given time. Divisions between Conservatives and Liberals before 1914 seemed very acute to contemporaries, but looked much less significant after 1918 when the two parties were confronted by the rapid advance of the Labour Party. A leading partisan of the earlier period could then comment:

> The questions which are coming up for a settlement are not those which divided the parties in pre-war days but are economic and social questions challenging the very basis of our national life and industry upon which the older parties have always been agreed. (quoted in Dutton, 1985, p. 222)

The whole basis of British politics is adversarial in structure, right down to the procedures and formal customs of parliamentary debate. Formal party political co-operation has been alien to the British system since 1945 except for the brief period of the Lib-Lab Pact in the late 1970s. The notion of 'confrontational' politics has enjoyed a recent vogue in describing the years of the Thatcher Government, but it is in fact an accurate description of the form (if not always the substance) of the modern British constitution as a whole. There is

3

always a danger in such a system that observers — and even perhaps participants — will allow the rhetoric and propaganda of party political battle to conceal the essential underlying continuities of a largely bipartisan approach. The British system encourages opposition for opposition's sake, but the ritual of aggrieved indignation is often little more than the necessary accompaniment of a well-structured political game. In a two-party system there is, after all, little to be gained by an opposition party stressing its agreement with government policy. If an electorate is to be offered good reasons for rejecting a government and installing an alternative party in office, it is the differences — no matter how marginal or even exaggerated — which must be emphasized, rather than the points of agreement. Without differences being highlighted a General Election becomes meaningless — simply a choice between more or less interchangeable sets of ministers. It was noticeable, for example, that the General Election of 1951 was among the most bitter and hard-fought of the postwar era, even though its outcome probably resulted in fewer changes of policy and direction than any other party political change-over of the same period.

Similar arguments apply to the position of the electorate. It is certainly true that the years of consensus were marked by a degree of consistent and passionate voter commitment unmatched in more recent times. Electors unhesitatingly proclaimed themselves Labour or Conservative in these years and the vast majority were unlikely ever to cross the dividing line between the two parties. Again, however, appearances may have been deceptive. We should be wary of attributing to the electorate either too high a degree of rationality in its voting decisions, or anything approaching a full knowledge of the party programmes on offer. Much of the strength of postwar party loyalty was founded upon deep-seated class consciousness and a family tradition of voting behaviour, both of which factors have diminished in importance in recent years.

Pimlott's idea that the 'consensus myth' is largely a product of a retrospective vision from the polarized era of Margaret Thatcher and Tony Benn is also open to question. As Pimlott himself recognizes, the seminal work in the development of the consensus theory, Paul Addison's *The Road to 1945*, was published in 1975, before the concept of 'Thatcherism' had begun to impinge on the political consciousness. Finally, Pimlott's argument that the existence of a consensus ought to have meant a strong centre party may be stood on its head. It was precisely the perceived moderation of the two leading parties which deprived the Liberals of any unique claim to occupy the centre ground in British politics. Not surprisingly, therefore, in the 1951 General Election the two main parties between them shared 96.8 per cent of the votes cast; in 1970 they still monopolized 91.5 per cent. It is surely instructive that the Liberal Party came close to disappearing within the Conservative ranks when Churchill formed his government in 1951, while just over a decade later there was serious talk of a realignment of the centre-left which might have seen Liberalism subsumed within the Labour Party of Gaitskell and Wilson. It was in fact the electorate's perception of the growing polarization of politics after about 1970, with the Conservatives moving to the right and Labour to the left, which left the centre ground vacant for a Liberal revival and even the temporary upsurge of a new force in the Social Democratic Party.

Professor Pimlott is not alone in questioning the consensus theory. Kevin Jefferys disputes the idea that a consensus had been formed by the end of the Second World War. Party politics were, he asserts, alive and well beneath a surface veneer of wartime unity. When the Churchill Coalition came to an end in May 1945, it had not effected a fundamental change in the domestic basis of British politics. 'Conflict rather than consensus was once more the natural order' (Jefferys, 1987a, p. 14). Peter Jenkins goes further, arguing that there never was a consensus (Jenkins, 1987, p. 4). He suggests that Britain suffered markedly from 'sharp and usually ideologically-inspired changes in direction' as a result of the alternation of Conservative and Labour governments after 1945 (Jenkins, 1987, p. 3). Yet, while he rejects the notion of a consensus, Jenkins is ready somewhat paradoxically to concede that what he calls a postwar 'settlement' did grow out of the war years, which set out 'not only the framework but the agenda for post-war politics' (Jenkins,

5

1987, p. 5). Roger Eatwell stresses that the level of consensus, either during the war or later, must not be overstated and that considerable ideological differences remained (Eatwell, 1979, p. 159). For Michael Fraser the reality is best expressed by seeing the Labour and Conservative parties as two trains starting off from parallel platforms, running for a while along broadly parallel lines 'but always heading for very different destinations' (Hennessy and Seldon, 1987, p. 310). David Marquand accepts that the parties argued out their differences and settled governmental policies within a framework of common commitments and assumptions, but regards 'consensus' as an imprecise term and warns that Labour and the Conservatives always differed profoundly about the details of policy, the source of political authority and the goals for which they were striving (Hennessy and Seldon, 1987, pp. 318–19). For Tony Benn, anxious always to support his argument that Labour governments have failed to deliver their promised goal of a socialist society, the postwar or 'welfare-capitalist' consensus is merely one consensus to be set alongside that which existed after the formation of the National Government in 1931 and what he describes as the 'monetarist' consensus which began when the Labour Government accepted the terms of the International Monetary Fund in 1976 (Hennessy and Seldon, 1987, p. 301).

These criticisms make it necessary to define precisely what is meant by the idea of a postwar consensus as the term will be used in this book. At one level an important political consensus has existed in this country throughout the present century. There has long been a wide-ranging consensus as to the legitimacy of the state and its constitutional apparatus – something which was markedly lacking in, for example, the early years of the Third Republic in France. Furthermore, our modern party system could not have been developed without a basic agreement between the parties over the rules by which they compete for power and govern the country. An adversarial system could not in practice exist unless a fair measure of common ground is maintained between those parties which alternate in government. Indeed, it is basic to the successful functioning of a two-party system that the contenders for power should not be at completely opposite ends of a political spectrum. Any given period tends to define for itself the range of policies which are capable of implementation, irrespective of the political colour of the party in power. Because political success within a democracy requires a party to appeal beyond its own natural constituency, there is an inherent tendency for all genuine aspirants for power to move towards the political centre. This was true even in the apparently polarized years between the two world wars. While Baldwin strove to contrast his Conservatives' 'national' appeal with Labour's, which he presented as 'sectional', Labour's primary concern in its two periods in power was to present itself as a moderate and responsible party of government.

Yet after 1945 the concept of consensus came to mean rather more. The rest of this book will focus on the idea that after 1945 the political parties operated within a given framework, a set of generally accepted parameters in which certain key assumptions were shared and in which policy options were consequently limited. Disputes were less about absolutes than questions of 'more' or 'less'. In brief, on the domestic front these shared assumptions included the provision by government of a wide-ranging welfare state; the maintenance — with government as the accepted agent — of a high and stable level of employment; and the continuing presence of a mixed economy. Abroad the consensus embraced a commitment to the collective defence of the West in partnership with the United States and against the Soviet Union, while maintaining Britain's independent status as a great power; and the progressive evolution of the dependent Empire into the voluntary association of the Commonwealth.

Consensus is not meant to imply total agreement, nor an unspoken coalition of policy and intention. It was never complete between the whole of the Labour and Conservative parties. Each represented, as it always had, a broad spectrum of opinion. Labour contained both social democrats and an avowedly socialist left wing; Conservatism combined a collectivist, paternalistic strain with a free-market, libertarian right. The extreme poles of the two parties remained irreconcilable and

7

could never be part of the consensus. What is important to note is that during the years under discussion it was the left wing of the Conservatives and the right of Labour which dominated their respective parties. The practical effect was a general convergence towards the centre ground of British politics. Bearing in mind what has been said already about the duty of opposition parties being to oppose, we may most clearly see the postwar consensus not in relation to the two political parties, nor even as between governments and oppositions, but in terms of the fundamental continuity between the governing elites of the two parties, alternating in power in succession to one another. It is in government that its practitioners learn that politics is indeed the art of the possible.

1

The Origins of the Consensus, 1940–45

For a long time – perhaps until the publication of Paul Addison's *The Road to 1945* – the Second World War was something of a backwater as far as British domestic political history was concerned. Attention focused, understandably enough, on the military and diplomatic history of these years, while the declaration of a party political truce as far as wartime by-elections were concerned and the formation of an all-party coalition in May 1940 gave the superficial impression that there were relatively few major domestic issues awaiting detailed historical attention. Yet changes in the political complexion of the country were clearly taking place, as the crushing defeat of Winston Churchill in the General Election of 1945 bears witness. The failure of Churchill, the great hero of the war effort, indeed the personification of the nation's resolve to resist Hitler's aggression, to cash in on the military victory secured in 1945 to the benefit of his own political party cannot simply be explained away as a delayed electoral condemnation of the failures, at home and abroad, of the Conservative-dominated National Government of the 1930s. Churchill's inability to repeat the experience of Lloyd George in 1918, and take the electorate by storm in 1945, can only be explained by fundamental changes in political attitudes during the war years themselves.

These changes took place at both an intellectual and a popular level. Among the electorate as a whole, the sacrifices

9

of the war years gave rise to heightened expectations about the securing of a better world when arms were finally laid down. In this respect the war was like its predecessor of 1914. But there were important differences. With government encouragement, the Second World War was seen as being fought for the benefit of the common man. It was a 'People's War' and it would be the people as a whole who would gain from ultimate victory. The ethos of the First World War had been altogether more conservative. In so far as the earlier war had promised improvements for the common man — 'a land fit for heroes to live in' — these had been largely disappointed. Yet as the Second World War progressed there developed an overwhelming determination that such disappointments should not be repeated. The second war also disrupted civilian society, with all its deep-rooted class-based structures, to a far greater degree than had its predecessor, adding further to the egalitarian thrust which it carried forward. Some observers were not slow to recognize that, whatever it did to Britain's position in the international arena, the war might become a catalyst for major social and political change. From the Labour left Aneurin Bevan wrote at the beginning of 1940:

> War opens minds that were sealed, stimulates dormant intelligences and recruits into political controversy thousands who otherwise would remain in the political hinterland. It is with these new, eager virgin minds that Labour must concern itself if it is to breast the tides of war and emerge from it holding the leadership of the nation. (quoted in Campbell, 1987, p. 94)

Even though the war failed to kindle the revolutionary socialist fervour for which Bevan longed, its impact was nonetheless profound.

The war inevitably changed people's perceptions of the proper role of government in society. The mobilization of a whole country for its supreme effort could not be, and was not, achieved using those techniques of *laissez-faire* and non-intervention which were still firmly entrenched in the govern-

10

mental ethos of the 1930s. What government had claimed to be impossible only a few years earlier — namely to manage the economy successfully and eliminate unemployment — now seemed practical and realistic. It is also important to note that the new functions assumed by government during the war were widely judged to have been a success. It seemed remarkable that the unemployment which had been regarded as an intractable scourge of earlier years had been eliminated. Likewise the enormous industrial contribution to the salvation of the nation in the crisis of 1940 and to ultimate victory five years later seemed beyond dispute. Now it is true that the economic and industrial achievements of wartime Britain have been trenchantly and persuasively challenged by the historian Correlli Barnett. He argues that total employment in all sectors of the productive economy did not in fact rise during the war, but actually fell by about 1.6 million (C. Barnett, 1986, p. 260). Furthermore, British industry continued to display many of the long-term symptoms of decay which would come home to roost when the war was over. Yet as far as the present argument is concerned the contemporary perception is probably more important than the reality. The organization of the home front for war became something of a model for the reorganization of the peace.

The war thus aroused exaggerated beliefs in the power of the state to control the economy and to cure unemployment — beliefs that would not go away when peace returned. Centralized planning would be the panacea for the nation's postwar problems, including the creation of a better and fairer society, just as it had solved the problems thrown up by the war. For the man in the street this amounted to a gut feeling that government should intervene beneficially in areas from which it had previously been excluded. At Whitehall and Westminster this feeling was increasingly underpinned by an intellectual acceptance of the ideas of the Cambridge economist, John Maynard Keynes. The war brought into the Civil Service large numbers of economists who had adopted Keynes's *General Theory of Employment, Interest and Money*, published in 1936, and who firmly believed that demand management of the economy was possible.

In a remarkably short period of time Keynesian economics became the accepted orthodoxy. The concepts of a large public sector, high state spending and a generally active government had been legitimized.

Keynesian economics are of intrinsic importance to the postwar consensus and some attempt at definition must be made. The task is not easy. According to an old jibe, whenever five economists are gathered together, there will be six opinions and two of them will derive from Keynes (Peden, 1988, p. 35). Certainly Keynes himself recognized that economics deals with changing problems within a changing environment. His own ideas were steadily modified through the 1920s, 1930s and early 1940s. Yet their application to the policies of successive governments was most loudly proclaimed in the twenty-five years after Keynes's death in 1946. Broadly speaking, Keynesian economics implied that governments should accept permanent responsibility for aggregate demand in the economy, so as to ensure full employment without creating a vicious spiral of wage-price inflation. Perhaps his most novel idea was to argue that governments should be ready to borrow to finance expenditure when the economy was working at below full capacity (Peden, 1988, pp. 10–11).

By the end of 1940 a broad alliance, not party political in nature, was taking shape in favour of postwar social reform. What held it together was a belief in the state's capacity to reduce social injustice and, by expanding the economy, to create a better life for the whole population. It was not necessary to be a socialist to believe that the poverty and injustices of the 1920s and 1930s should be eliminated when peace returned. A special edition of the magazine *Picture Post* in January 1941 showed how far the commitment to a planned society had taken root. In it the architect Maxwell Fry pronounced that when rebuilding began the new Britain would have to be planned. His message was echoed by the economist, Thomas Balogh, who promised that a planned economy would lead to full employment. To complete the vision A. D. Lindsay, the Master of Balliol, Julian Huxley, the scientist, and J. B. Priestley, novelist and broadcaster, sketched their plans for education, health and leisure in postwar Britain. Priestley had already become a national figure as a result of his Sunday evening talks on the BBC. His central message was that there could be no going back to the social conditions of the 1930s (Addison, 1975, p. 118).

These developments need to be set against a background of important political changes which were taking place at the same time, though largely independently of them. In May 1940 Chamberlain's Conservative-dominated National Government fell from power to be replaced by a genuinely all-party coalition led by Winston Churchill. In this government most of the important posts on the domestic front were occupied by senior figures from the Labour Party. Indeed, with the exceptions of Anthony Eden and Churchill himself, the war failed to throw up many major new faces in the Conservative Party to replace that generation which had largely disappeared with Chamberlain as the 'Guilty Men' of the previous decade. Three key appointments should be noted. Clement Attlee, leader of the Labour Party, became Lord Privy Seal and later Deputy Prime Minister. In practice he increasingly emerged as the most powerful figure on the home front, allowing Churchill to concentrate on the diplomatic and military aspects of the war effort. In an inspired move Churchill appointed Ernest Bevin, General Secretary of the Transport and General Workers' Union, as Minister of Labour. As such Bevin assumed crucial powers over the industrial labour force. During the war the trade unions developed a status in society that they had never previously enjoyed, and it was Bevin's presence which ensured that this new role should far outlast the ending of the war. Herbert Morrison had the chance to display his administrative skills as Minister of Supply and later Home Secretary. These men emerged as respected and successful figures in the public mind and it was in the domestic ministries which they headed and the cabinet committees which they dominated that thought was given, at a governmental level, to the sort of society which should emerge when the war was over. The respective priorities of the two main parties within the government had important implications. While Churchill strove to win, Labour strove to win something beyond mere victory. This, of course, is a rather crude generalization. But it was also a clear perception in the eyes of the electorate.

On the whole the Coalition Cabinet functioned well. This is not to imply, of course, that there were no important disagreements within the government. But such differences of opinion are the very stuff of cabinet government, even in one of a single party. The glare of publicity and the propensity of recent cabinets to 'leak' information once regarded as confidential makes this abundantly clear to the contemporary observer, but it has always been the case. Yet an Australian observer of the Churchill Government noted that 'practically all the Labour Ministers integrate loyally and helpfully with the Tories, particularly Bevin' (quoted in Pelling, 1984, p. 18). Attlee himself frequently emphasized the amount of common ground which existed between the major parties. This was not altogether surprising, for by 1940 the leading figures in the Labour Party had come a long way from the woolly idealism which had characterized Labour thinking during the early 1930s. Inspired by Keynes's *General Theory*, they had come to re-examine the prospect of a Labour government trying to work within a healthy capitalist system. Their revolutionary days, if they had ever existed, were a thing of the past (Eatwell, 1979, p. 28).

Political developments in the government and changes in popular expectation among the nation at large came together as the Coalition itself helped to heighten public expectations about the postwar world with a series of officially sponsored blueprints for reconstruction. Of these the most important was undoubtedly the Beveridge Report of 1942. This milestone in social planning proposed that existing schemes of welfare support should be consolidated into a universal national scheme. Beveridge argued that the success of a future social security system would also involve the introduction of family allowances, the creation of a national health service and the maintenance of a high level of employment. This was not the blueprint for a socialist state. Indeed, it is worth pointing out that Beveridge himself was essentially a non-party figure, although he stood unsuccessfully as a Liberal in the General Election of 1945. The author of this great plan was perhaps more interested in social administration than social welfare and in institutions rather than people. The plan represented the coming together of existing pressures for a more progressive capitalism. Its timing was significant. Coming shortly after the victory at El Alamein, acceptance of Beveridge was almost synonymous with faith in victory and belief in a fair division of the fruits of that victory. The plan's impact and popular acclaim were such that the leading political parties had to accept it as the basis of the postwar society which one of them would have to build.

That acceptance was definite, if not of uniform intensity. On the Conservative benches there were certainly many who were as yet reluctant to envisage the sort of society which Beveridge proclaimed. More importantly, leading Conservatives in the government were hesitant on two grounds. Churchill in particular believed that one job should be tackled at a time. For the moment that job was to win the war. Discussions on the shape of postwar society were at best premature, but possibly also dangerous since they might divert attention from the immediate crisis, whose resolution was as yet by no means settled. If the military tide had begun to turn in Britain's favour after the defeats of earlier years, the transformation was far from complete. There was also a financial argument and the problem of raising public expectations which could not be met. Churchill had been in politics long enough to recall the mood of bitterness and disappointment when the 1920s failed to deliver the better world promised during the previous war. His Chancellor of the Exchequer, Kingsley Wood, warned that the Beveridge scheme, though largely based on contributions, would rely heavily on a deficiency grant from general taxation 'which will grow in the course of time to immense proportions' (quoted in C. Barnett, 1986, p. 47). The basic costs of postwar reconstruction might well pose an acute strain on the national economy without superimposing the burdens of an advanced scheme of social security. The Treasury was anxious that no particular commitments should be entered into until a clearer picture emerged of the country's likely financial burden as a whole.

Such thinking determined the rather reserved stance adopted by the government when the House of Commons came to debate the Beveridge Plan in February 1943. It also explains why ninety-seven Labour members — virtually the whole of the party outside the Coalition Government — decided to defy their leadership and call for much earlier legislation than the government wanted. This outcome was doubly significant. On the one hand there seems little doubt that both parties were now committed to a postwar welfare state. Indeed, to reassure the public Churchill broadcast to the nation on 21 March 1943 and proclaimed that the members of the government were 'strong partisans of national compulsory insurance for all classes for all purposes from the cradle to the grave' (quoted in Addison, 1975, p. 227). In economic matters his tone seemed distinctly Keynesian. Unemployment would be prevented by government action to 'exercise a balancing influence upon development which can be turned on or off as circumstances require'. He even seemed ready to envisage an extended measure of state ownership. On the other hand, the public perception was that Labour was the party most likely to turn Beveridge's plans into postwar reality. The overall Conservative embrace of Beveridge seemed short on passion and conviction.

Such an analysis was not entirely fair. It is interesting that Beveridge himself had suggested that a Conservative government would be the best vehicle for carrying through his policies, while even Attlee suspected that the reason for Churchill's present caution was his determination to take personal credit for the implementation of the Beveridge proposals as the head of a postwar Conservative administration (Harris, 1982, p. 220). Although Conservative enthusiasts for Beveridge were probably in a minority, a group of about fifty MPs in the newly formed Tory Reform Committee led by Quintin Hogg and Lord Hinchingbrooke called for the immediate creation of a Ministry of Social Security. This group kept up pressure on the party leadership to adopt a more positive attitude towards the Plan and enjoyed some success. Labour's Hugh Dalton noted that the Tory Reform Committee 'would be quite prepared for a continuance of controls, for much state action and some state ownership' (Pimlott, 1986, p. 597).

The Beveridge Report was only the most important of a series of such planning documents produced during the years of the Churchill Coalition. A Cabinet Committee on Reconstruction was set up in 1943 and reached broad agreement on social security, education, child allowances and Keynesian budgetary management. White papers soon followed. *Educational Reconstruction* was published in July 1943. It proposed a universal system of secondary education and prepared the way for the Education Act of 1944. Though recent research has shown that R. A. Butler, the Conservative President of the Board of Education, was often at odds on points of detail with his Labour deputy, James Chuter Ede, this should not blind us to the fundamental cross-party consensus which had emerged on questions of education (Jeffreys, 1987a). As *The Times* pointed out, during the two-day debate on the government's white paper, 'not a single voice was raised in favour of holding up or whittling down any of the proposals for educational advance.' Later controversy on the issue of comprehensive schools can too easily obscure the widespread support, lasting until the 1960s, for the principles enshrined in Butler's Act, including the segregation of eleven-year-olds into grammar, secondary modern and technical education.

In February 1944 the government produced *A National Health Service*, which envisaged a free and comprehensive service to cover every branch of medicine. Then, almost as important as the Beveridge Report itself, came a white paper on employment policy in May 1944. Its opening sentence would be engrained upon the hearts and indeed the manifestos of Conservative and Labour governments for the next thirty years. It would be the duty of governments to maintain 'a high and stable level of employment'. Some Tories were known to have considerable doubts about the feasibility of this far-reaching commitment. The new party chairman, Ralph Assheton, was among the sceptics. But once again there was a bipartisan consensus as far as the front benches of the two parties were concerned.

17

It was an agreement which greatly disturbed the socialist, Aneurin Bevan. In *Why not Trust the Tories?* (1944) Bevan condemned the white paper as a surrender to market forces and capitalism. In Parliament he noted:

> The question of how the work of society is to be organised, how the income of society is to be distributed, to what extent the State is to intervene in the direction of economic affairs — all these are questions which first called this party into existence. They represent in themselves the main bone of contention between the main parties in the State. How on earth therefore can a Coalition Government pretend to approach these problems without the gravest sacrifice of principles? . . . if the implications of the White Paper are sound, there is no longer any justification for this Party existing at all. (quoted in Campbell, 1987, p. 130)

Bevan's comments are important. They emphasize that the new consensus — and the basis of the postwar Labour Government's domestic policies — was in no sense socialist. It is perhaps best seen as the expression of a 'mildly interventionist social democracy', which would later be described as 'Butskellism'. It owed far more to Keynes than to Marx (Campbell, 1987, p. 144).

One policy area where inter-party differences remained was the future ownership of British industry. The Conservatives set their faces against formal nationalization; by 1945 it was an important part of Labour's programme. Yet, even in this field, the party divisions should not be overstated. Though the word 'nationalization' remained anathema to them, many Conservatives, as well as leading industrialists, envisaged greater state regulation when the war was over. Coal provides an interesting example. The Coalition Government was committed to continuing state authority in its management, with reserve powers to effect compulsory amalgamations. The Tory Reform Committee went one step further, condemning the existing structure of the industry in 1944 and calling for a reduction in the number of companies to around fifty and the introduction of regional planning (Addison, 1985, p. 180).

The general thrust of wartime developments had been in a leftward direction, towards a vaguely progressive future, but it had been carried on a tide which had taken all parties along with it. As Attlee told Harold Laski in 1944, whichever party was in power after the war, it would have to work in a mixed economy (Harris, 1982, p. 254). The effective result, therefore, was to relocate the centre ground of British politics much further to the left than it had been in the 1930s. What might have appeared mildly revolutionary in 1939 had, only six years later, become an entirely natural evolution. Attlee was stunned at 'the extent to which what we cried in the wilderness five and twenty years ago has now become part of the assumptions of the ordinary man and woman' (quoted in Burridge, 1985, p. 140). But as the moment approached for the electorate to install a party government in power once more, Labour was uniquely linked in the popular mind with the new social agenda that had emerged. By comparison many Conservatives seemed to have been driven helplessly along on the prevailing tide, 'apprehensively dropping anchor in strange Keynesian waters' (Addison, 1975, p. 166).

At the defeat of Germany Churchill gave to each of the party leaders within the wartime coalition the option of remaining in the government until the end of the Japanese war or else of withdrawing immediately so that an election could be held in July 1945. Attlee expressed a preference for an autumn election, an option which Churchill had not offered. Accordingly, the country went to the polls in July. Interestingly, R. A. Butler later recalled that he had wanted the coalition to continue at least until Japan had been beaten and 'preferably until the social reforms upon which we were in general agreement had been passed' (R. A. Butler, 1971, pp. 126–7).

Labour's overwhelming victory in the General Election of 1945 looks much less surprising after the passage of nearly half a century than it did at the time. In one sense there was little to choose between the two main parties — except, of course, that

19

the one was led by the towering personality of Winston Churchill. Both shared — as did the Liberals — a common commitment to the programme of reconstruction worked out between 1942 and 1945. The Conservative manifesto, *Mr. Churchill's Declaration of Policy to the Electors*, pledged the party to implement Beveridge, to carry out the provisions of Butler's Education Act, to set up some sort of national health service, to embark on a major homebuilding programme and to maintain a high and stable level of employment. Labour, of course, was committed to these same goals and also to the traditionally Tory aim of ensuring that Britain remained a major world power, one of the Big Three with the United States and the Soviet Union, and at the head of the Empire. Public ownership was an area of dispute, but even here it was significant that Labour argued its case pragmatically, usually in terms of promoting greater industrial efficiency. Nationalization was not presented as an ideological crusade. What was significant, however, was the scale of priority given to their various pledges by the two parties and the intensity with which they were presented to the electorate.

It was noticeable that statements on foreign policy came at the beginning of the Conservative manifesto and at the end of Labour's. But it was in the handling of the respective campaigns that the differences appeared most clearly to the electorate. Labour's focus was simply and emphatically upon the material needs of the ordinary family. Its message exuded moderation. Labour wanted to consolidate the achievements of the wartime consensus, to maintain the system of state planning which the war had created. The Conservative campaign stressed the problems which still lay ahead and was often negative and divisive, particularly after Churchill entered the fray. Butler later admitted that it would have been better if the Conservatives had not placed their commitments to postwar reconstruction a poor third behind the exploitation of Churchill's personality and a negative attack on the Labour Party (R. A. Butler, 1971, p. 128). Even Harold Macmillan from the Conservatives' left wing sounded cautious, with only guarded enthusiasm for the New Jerusalem ahead:

In the realm of national economic planning we shall hold a wise balance between the field suited for private enterprise and that allocated for ownership or control ... the Government will follow the national characteristic − a middle course avoiding equally the extreme of laissez-faire and that of collectivist control for its own sake. (Horne, 1988, p. 284)

The fact was that progressive Tories had failed to persuade the majority of their colleagues to adopt the details of the wartime consensus as their electoral battle-cry. The coalition programme was accepted by many with only lukewarm commitment. 'If you do not give the people social reform,' Quintin Hogg had warned the House of Commons, 'they are going to give you social revolution' (quoted in Addison, 1975, p. 232). In practice the consequence was nearer to a political revolution, with the election of a majority Labour Government for the first time in the country's history with a massive parliamentary majority of 146 seats over all other parties combined.

2

The Foundation of the Consensus, 1945–51

The Labour governments of 1945–51 have been well served by their historians (particularly Morgan, 1984; Pelling, 1984; Harris, 1982; Bullock, 1983). Even so, they retain an enigmatic quality. Until fairly recent times there was at least a general recognition of the importance of their achievements, though the nature of those achievements was open to debate. Even Conservatives, notwithstanding a token genuflection to adversarial opposition, viewed these years with a grudging respect. Among Labour supporters in general there was none of the tendency, so marked after the later governments of 1964–70 and 1974–79, to denigrate the achievements of Attlee's administration or to distance themselves from its record. The two dominant Labour figures of the 1950s, Hugh Gaitskell on the right and Aneurin Bevan on the left, could both look back to the Attlee years with a sense of pride and satisfaction. But it remained open to question whether Labour partisans held the Attlee Government in such esteem because it saw the only significant stride which Labour has ever taken towards the establishment of a socialist state, or because it marked Labour's firm entrenchment on the path of non-ideological social democracy. Yet in recent years a more critical commentary has become apparent. Tony Benn's assessment that 1945 marked the beginning of a 'welfare-capitalist consensus' has already been noted. For the New Right Conservatives of the 1970s and

1980s, 1945 inaugurated thirty years of collectivism and bureaucratic centralism. In this period the Conservative Party was shifted progressively in a socialistic direction by what Keith Joseph saw as a ratchet effect, while the country slid inexorably into deep decline before the rescue operation launched by Margaret Thatcher after 1979.

The character of the postwar Labour Government is clearly of intrinsic importance to the argument of this book. For if the Attlee Government really did mark the implementation of left-wing socialism, the thesis of a moderate postwar consensus growing out of the years of war falls to the ground. It will be argued that the major achievement of the Labour Party after 1945 was to complete and consolidate the work of the wartime coalition. The changes which the government introduced fell far short of a social or economic revolution. As in 1964 and 1974, though perhaps with greater competence, Labour set out to make the capitalist system work. The class structure of the country was hardly affected and there was no significant redistribution of the nation's wealth. Most of the government's measures were far less distasteful to the Conservative Party than was sometimes claimed. This is not to say that a Conservative government in 1945, especially one headed by Winston Churchill, would have pursued an almost identical course. Some clear differences would have been evident. But a Conservative government would have proceeded along very similar lines and operated within comparable parameters.

The moderation of the Labour Government clearly requires some words of explanation. In the first place, its leadership was firmly planted in the centre, if not the right, of the Labour movement. The Big Four of 1945, Attlee (Prime Minister), Morrison (Lord President), Bevin (Foreign Secretary) and Dalton (Chancellor), were cautious and responsible politicians who had all served a governmental apprenticeship under Churchill during the war. Attlee was completely wedded to the parliamentary system and, whatever he may have believed earlier in his career, content to work within a mixed economy of reformed capitalism. If a genuinely socialist society was ever to be created, such an event lay far off in the future. The duration

23

of the period of transition could not even be predicted. Though the parliament elected in 1945 contained much socialist idealism, the harsh practicalities of postwar reconstruction served greatly to temper unrealistic aspirations. By 1948 Harold Macmillan could note, with some concern for its impact on the Tory Party, that 'the Labour movement as a whole is turning towards the centre' (quoted in Horne, 1988, p. 300).

Beneath the Big Four many other leading ministers displayed similar moderation. At the Ministry of Defence, A. V. Alexander was almost an old-fashioned imperialist. The Home Secretary, Chuter Ede, exuded caution. Successive Ministers of Education, Ellen Wilkinson and George Tomlinson, were not likely to foster any sweeping changes. The left wing was represented in the cabinet by Aneurin Bevan and Emanuel Shinwell, although the latter could on occasions be remarkably conservative. Bevan had his hands full at the Ministry of Health and was effectively excluded from the determination of the main thrust of the government's programme. Shinwell, too, exerted little overall influence. 'The Attlee government', concludes its leading historian, 'does not emerge on the whole as a body of committed or instinctive radicals' (Morgan, 1984, p. 56). It was this government which, when confronted by a dock strike within weeks of taking office, re-enacted the detested Emergency Powers Act of 1920, with even Ernest Bevin, former General Secretary of the Transport and General Workers' Union, concurring.

Even had the leading members of the Labour Government been more inclined to embark on a socialist crusade, the circumstances of the time would have conspired to constrain them. All governments are subject to, indeed sometimes prisoners of, a prevailing climate – political, diplomatic, economic and social – over which they have only limited control. This is particularly true in relation to overseas factors impinging upon Britain's position. But the postwar Labour Government was more than usually restricted in its freedom of manoeuvre. The fundamental fact of life in 1945 was that Britain was all but bankrupt. During the course of the war Britain had lost about a quarter of its entire national wealth. The financial and economic

24

legacy of the struggle against Hitler was almost unendurable. The combination of lost overseas assets, a massive trade imbalance, lost markets, a shortage of raw materials and an enormous dollar deficit would take many years to overcome. The government, presented by Keynes with the grim realities of the situation in its first week in office, made the acquisition of a loan from the United States in the order of five billion dollars its first priority. Though not all realized it at the time, the basic pattern of the government's affairs had thus been fixed.

Labour's six years in power were marked by continuous domestic economic difficulties. In addition, the government was constantly mindful of the need to avoid damaging the country's exports, to maintain confidence in sterling and not to endanger continued American generosity in terms of loans and aid. The last factor was perhaps the most important of all. Without the inflow of American cash Britain would have faced conditions of extreme austerity and the most cherished of Labour's designs, the Welfare State, would scarcely have got off the ground. The party's left wing, largely removed from the responsible seats of power, often overestimated the relatively narrow scope of choice open to the government.

This situation determined Labour's approach to the general management of the national economy. The environment of internal and external crises ruled out any real prospect of socialist planning of the country's production. There were some moves early on, especially in the Steering Committee on Economic Policy, towards long-term macro-economic planning, but these were short-lived and did not really survive the end of Dalton's Chancellorship in 1947. According to his biographer, Dalton's resignation symbolized 'the end of the radical phase and the start of a period of compromise and consolidation' (Pimlott, 1985, p. 536). Even under Dalton, Labour's efforts to plan the private sector via the Treasury and the Board of Trade were half-hearted and not particularly successful. From 1948 the physical controls on investment and the use of raw materials were progressively dismantled. Sir Stafford Cripps, Chancellor from 1947 to 1950, has been described as beginning the long reign of Keynesians at 11 Downing Street which lasted perhaps until 1979 (Morgan, 1984, p. 364). Under him the vague commitment to centralized economic planning was abandoned, apart from the setting of optimistic targets. An economic strategy took its place which would dominate the Treasury's thinking until the 1970s. As a Treasury mandarin of the time commented: 'The last government adopted in 1947 and 1948 a revolution in British practice, when they took responsibility for maintaining full employment but avoiding inflation' (quoted in Morgan, 1984, p. 364). Symbolic of the change was the so-called 'bonfire of controls' inaugurated by Harold Wilson, the President of the Board of Trade, in November 1948. Though the Conservatives would later be elected on the slogan of 'setting the people free', most of the work had already been done for them before they entered office. By the time of Cripps's last budget in 1950 *The Times* could comment that Labour had finally made the transition from idealistic theory to common sense. The actual experience of government had proved 'a graveyard of doctrine' and, in an important sense, a barrier had been erected between the Labour Party and the economic theories of Marxism (Harris, 1982, p. 452).

If one socialist beacon shone forth from the Labour Government's otherwise orthodox economic record, it was surely its policy of nationalization. Here was a practical response to the commitment entered into through its socialist constitution back in 1918. Yet a number of qualifications must be made. In the first place, the general concept of public ownership was not new, as the establishment of the Port of London Authority in 1909 and the Central Electricity Board and the British Broadcasting Corporation in 1926 bear witness. The war, of course, had provided many examples of governmental control of industry, and the widespread readiness to see such practices continue into the peace showed that nationalization was not primarily envisaged as dogmatic socialism. Many industrialists and managers, traditional supporters of the Conservative Party, were convinced by the experience of the war that a measure of state control was necessary. They were ready to support the compul-

26

sory reorganization of certain key industries, particularly in fuel and transport, which would be vital for postwar reconstruction.

Labour's nationalization programme was largely the responsibility of Herbert Morrison and it is striking that he sought to justify each measure on its merits as a way of improving the efficiency and usefulness of the industry concerned. It was in these terms that nationalization was presented in Labour's 1945 manifesto, *Let Us Face the Future*. Indeed, this document preferred to use the term 'public ownership' rather than 'nationalization'. Thus an economic rather than a political or social justification predominated in Labour's rhetoric. This fact determined the rather narrow range of industries which came into public ownership during the lifetime of the Labour Government. The chief elements in Labour's programme were the Bank of England (1946), coal (1947), electricity (1948), gas (1948) and the railways (1948). Nor did Morrison envisage the programme of 1945 as merely the beginning of a longer-term or more wide-ranging assault on private industry. It is striking that the policy document *Labour Believes in Britain*, published in 1949, marked 'an evident downgrading of the standing of nationalisation in Labour's future priorities' (Morgan, 1984, p. 123). Thus the industries encompassed in Labour's vision were 'either public utilities or ailing concerns of little value to their owners and no interest to other capitalists' (Addison, 1975, p. 273). The main exception was the commitment to nationalize the steel industry. Significantly, steel had been included in Labour's shopping list at the insistence of the Party Conference in 1944, but against the advice of Morrison and Arthur Greenwood. This was the one case where Labour did seem ready to tackle 'the commanding heights of the economy'. Its inclusion was more overtly ideological than any other nationalization measure which Labour undertook.

Most of the private sector of British industry, particularly its profitable parts, remained untouched by Labour's plans. The most that the government aspired to was a loose partnership with industry — one in which the forces of capital and the market would remain supreme. The form generally taken by those industries which were nationalized is also worthy of note.

It was that of the public corporation. This involved the creation of no new relationship between capital and labour. All that effectively happened was that the state bought out the existing ownership while allowing the existing management to remain in its place.

These factors determined the reaction of the Conservative Opposition to Labour's programme. Significantly, Harold Macmillan once commented of Morrison that on the question of the nationalization of public utilities, railways and the coal industry, 'our views were not very far apart' (Horne, 1988, p. 258). Less progressive Tories than Macmillan no doubt felt a gut revulsion against the whole concept, but the behaviour of the Opposition front bench is instructive. Attlee later recalled that, with the exception of steel, there was 'not much real opposition to our nationalization policy' (Attlee, 1954, p. 165). Labour's first measure, the nationalization of the Bank of England, was carried without controversy. Churchill said that the measure did not involve 'any issue of principle'. Conservatives were relieved that Labour was not proposing to shackle the main clearing banks or to try to control the movement of capital. The case of coal was not dissimilar. Wartime plans had envisaged some form of state control and though the Conservatives voted against the second reading of the bill, neither Churchill nor Eden offered more than token resistance in the Commons debate. On other measures the Conservatives put up a stiffer fight. The Transport Bill, covering road haulage, was vigorously opposed, as was that dealing with electricity. Though the Conservatives had accepted the report of the Heyworth Committee, recommending the public ownership of the gas industry, this did not stop them from putting down more than 800 amendments before the government's bill received the royal assent in July 1948. Even so, Labour's legislation was reformist and, in the circumstances of postwar Britain, not particularly controversial. The impression is that the Opposition's resistance was largely tactical and that, had they been in power in these years, some form of public ownership might still have resulted.

In the case of the steel industry it was a different story, and it is noticeable that opponents of the consensus thesis often fall back on this example to support their case. Over the period covered by this book steel was nationalized twice and denationalized (or privatized) twice. In this instance three factors are important. First, here Labour did seem to be crossing the important frontier between nationalization as a practical economic measure and nationalization as part of an overtly political objective. Second, the Labour leadership itself seemed unenthusiastic about its own proposals. The steel nationalization bill proposed to take over companies *en bloc* without reorganization or restructuring, thus making it relatively easy for a future Conservative government to denationalize the industry. And third, the timetable of Labour's crowded legislative programme ensured that steel became an election issue, where the Conservatives could call on the support of their traditional allies in industry and commerce, as the parliament of 1945 inexorably ran its course.

If its nationalization programme will not wholly sustain its socialist credentials, the left-wing admirers of the 1945 government would probably point to its social policy, and particularly the setting up of the National Health Service in 1948, as corroborative evidence. Once again, however, it is clear that, at least in general terms, much of the groundwork had been carried out by Churchill's coalition. This was particularly the case in relation to James Griffiths's National Insurance Bill, although the Labour Cabinet did decide to increase the scale of benefits previously proposed. The Conservative Opposition decided not to oppose the bill on second or third reading in the Commons. It was noticeable that the whole scheme was established on a sound actuarial basis. Benefits were not linked to the cost of living and any individual was free to take out additional cover from private insurance companies.

Only in the area of the National Health Service is there really scope for suggesting that Labour's enactments went significantly further than a Conservative government would have progressed. The Health Service is widely seen as a legislative memorial to Aneurin Bevan, the most avowedly socialist member of Attlee's cabinet. According to Kenneth Morgan, 'the National

Health Service is a prime exhibit in illustrating the danger of making too much of the continuity between the social consensus of the war years and the post-war Labour welfare state' (Morgan, 1984, p. 154). He argues that the ideas drawn up in 1944 by Henry Willink, Churchill's Minister of Health, fell short of Bevan's proposals in certain key areas, especially hospitals and health centres, and that a Conservative government would have introduced a much less ambitious scheme. It is, of course, impossible to prove what a postwar Conservative government would or would not have done. But other historians have been rather less convinced of the uniqueness of Bevan's achievement. Addison asserts that 'it is as certain as anything can be that a post-war Conservative government would have [established], in some form, a national health service' (Hennessy and Seldon, 1987, p. 14). It should be stressed that the basic idea of a comprehensive national health service was not new. Inter-war reports, such as the Dawson Report of 1920 and the Royal Commission on National Health Insurance in 1926, had pointed towards such a conclusion. It became a definite prospect with the acceptance of 'Assumption B' of the Beveridge Report in 1943. But, even before Beveridge, discussions had been going on inside the Ministry of Health, headed first by the Liberal National, Ernest Brown, and then the Conservative, Willink. All political parties accepted that the postwar parliament, whatever its political complexion, would introduce some scheme of comprehensive health cover. The British Medical Association itself was putting forward proposals, as were the leading medical journals, including *The Lancet*.

Bevan himself seems to have exaggerated his own achievement. His abrasive style and confrontational tactics were such as to create the impression of an heroic struggle, successfully carried out in the face of adversity and opposition. Bevan strove to make as much party political capital out of his creation as he possibly could. But the Minister's greatest battle was fought less with the Conservative Opposition than with the British Medical Association, though the Conservatives took up the doctors' cause in the House of Commons. It is instructive that when Attlee proposed to make a broadcast in which he would describe the NHS as a national achievement to which all parties had contributed, Bevan objected forcefully. Just before the Health Service came into operation Bevan made his notorious speech in Manchester in which he described the Tories as 'lower than vermin'. 'It seems clear', writes his latest biographer, 'that Bevan privately welcomed . . . the B.M.A's help in making the N.H.S. appear a more socialist measure than it really was' (Campbell, 1987, p. 179). Disappointed at the lack of socialist content in the rest of the government's policies, Bevan took comfort in the free Health Service, 'elevated into the touchstone of socialism' (Campbell, 1987, p. 149).

Most of the rest of Labour's domestic programme followed the same pattern. Education may be taken as an example, since it was an important element in the wartime consensus, while becoming a matter of inter-party dispute in the 1960s. The main task of Labour's minister, Ellen Wilkinson, was to put into operation a piece of legislation which was already on the statute book − Butler's Act of 1944. Her aim was to make secondary modern schools as good as grammar schools, but the pursuit of equality did not to her imply treating different people in the same way. As a grammar school product herself, and far less radical in her outlook that she had been in the 1930s, Wilkinson had little sympathy for the view which enjoyed some support in left-wing circles, that the Butler scheme was socially and educationally divisive. Her successor from 1947, George Tomlinson, made no fundamental change in the thrust of government policy.

The realm of foreign policy provides perhaps the clearest evidence of the centrist position occupied by Attlee's government. Paradoxically this was an area where, despite a long tradition of bipartisanship, Labour activists expected that the policies to be pursued by their government would be distinctly different from those which could be expected from a Conservative administration. The notion of a socialist foreign policy was in common currency in 1945, although precisely what it would mean in practice was not clear. Earlier Labour governments could be forgiven for their failure to adopt a distinctive approach because of their lack of a parliamentary majority, but no such impediment existed now. Whatever a socialist foreign policy might entail, it was certain that the Labour Government could be expected to build on the close wartime ties with the Soviet Union, whose standing in popular esteem, particularly as a result of the heroic exploits of the Red Army, had never been higher throughout that regime's history. For many years to come Labour activists would recall Ernest Bevin's promise given during the election campaign that 'left could speak with left' in comradeship and confidence, even though Bevin had probably had Anglo-French rather than Anglo-Soviet relations in mind.

Yet, as Denis Healey wrote in 1952, 'an understanding of the power element in politics is the first necessity for a sound foreign policy' (quoted in James, 1972, p. 59). Diplomacy is a far harder field than domestic politics for any given government to chart a distinctive course in, because more of the basic determinants lie outside the control of so-called policy-makers. This was particularly true in 1945. The pattern of wartime great power relations unfolded inexorably towards the new conflict of the Cold War, a conflict in which Britain's position was never seriously in doubt, if for no other reason than her total dependence on American financial support. Ernest Bevin, a surprise appointment to the Foreign Office (Dalton had expected to get the job), exercised a dominant and all-important influence over British diplomacy for the greater part of the duration of the Attlee Government, and succeeded in laying down a framework of policy which would form the basis of Britain's overseas relations under successive governments of differing political complexions for many years to come.

As soon as he had taken up the seals of office Bevin was thrown into the fray of great power relations as he and Attlee travelled to Potsdam to take over the seats of Eden and Churchill at the resumed Big Three Conference. The observation of the American Secretary of State, James Byrnes, is revealing: 'Britain's stand on the issues before the conference was not altered in the slightest, so far as we could discern, by the replacement of Mr. Churchill and Mr. Eden by Mr. Attlee and Mr. Bevin' (Byrnes, 1947, p. 79). This was not altogether surprising. Bevin was a hard-headed politician, whose earlier trade union career had left him with no love of Communism. Perhaps his major political contribution of the 1930s had been to help disabuse the Labour Party of its more idealistic fantasies and anchor its thinking firmly in the real world. During the war he had no doubt soaked up many of Churchill's foreign policy attitudes and beliefs, including his fundamental mistrust of Soviet Russia. Bevin's eminently practical attitude is well illustrated in this judgement of Molotov, his Soviet opposite number: 'If you treated him badly he made the most of his grievance and if you treated him well he only put up his price and abused you next day' (quoted in Sked and Cook, 1979, p. 54).

If Bevin had nurtured any fond hopes of cooperating successfully with Stalin's Russia, these could not have lasted long. Indeed, recent research suggests that Bevin's greatest achievement was to open the eyes of the United States to the reality of the Soviet menace and to secure an American protective role in recognition of Britain's incapacity, standing alone, to shoulder the burden of anti-Soviet defence (Bullock, 1983, pp. 839–48). By the time of the Foreign Ministers' Conference in Moscow in March 1947, Bevin and his American opposite number, George Marshall, were in substantial agreement on all important questions. Thereafter the government's absorption into the 'economic, political and military orbit of the United States became ever more explicit', particularly after the Czech coup of February 1948 and the Berlin blockade four months later (Morgan, 1984, p. 277).

The consistently anti-Soviet stance in Bevin's foreign policy provoked more disquiet on Labour's benches than any other aspect of the government's policies and programme. The foreign policy amendment to the Address in November 1946 was the most striking example, the emergence of the 'Keep Left' group a poignant reminder, of the extent to which the Foreign Secretary was deviating from the paths of true socialism. But, in the face of repeated illustrations of Soviet aggression and treachery, it became difficult for all but the most overt fellow-travellers in Labour's ranks to hold out against the logic of Bevin's stance. By early 1947 the vast majority of Labour MPs accepted Bevin's diagnosis of irreconcilable Soviet hostility towards the United Kingdom. As one diplomat noted of a foreign affairs debate in June 1947, 'the whole House was soberly anti-Russian' (quoted in Morgan, 1984, p. 261).

It is striking how many momentous decisions were taken during Bevin's Foreign Secretaryship. This was the government which determined in January 1947, albeit without full Cabinet consultation, that Britain should build its own atomic bomb. Two months later a National Service Bill was introduced to provide for peacetime conscription, while during the Berlin airlift of 1948 the government agreed to the siting of long-range American atomic bombers on British soil. Then in 1949 Britain became a founder member of NATO − very much a personal achievement of Ernest Bevin and, from that day to this, the basis of the country's foreign and defence policies. In 1950 Britain proved a loyal ally of the United States in the Korean War.

In the circumstances it was scarcely surprising that Bevin's foreign policy proved largely uncontentious as far as the Conservative Opposition was concerned. Bevin and Eden, his Conservative predecessor, got on well together and continued to engage in private consultation after the end of the coalition. 'I would publicly have agreed with him more', Eden later wrote, 'if I had not been anxious to embarrass him less' (Eden, 1960, p. 5). It was certainly true that the repeated endorsement of a Labour Foreign Secretary's policies from the parliamentary Opposition and the right-wing press was galling for left-wingers. Butler, too, recorded that 'on the major public issues arising from the cold war there was rarely much between us save a difference of emphasis or detail' (R. A. Butler, 1971, p. 131).

The foreign policy consensus extended beyond the central questions of Anglo-American and Anglo-Soviet relations. Fundamental to the Labour Government's approach was its acceptance as axiomatic that Britain remained one of the world's great powers. Of the decision to construct an atomic bomb, Margaret Gowing has written that it was a response to 'a feeling that Britain as a great power must acquire all major new weapons, a feeling that atomic weapons were a manifestation of

34

the scientific and technological superiority on which Britain's strength . . . must depend' (Gowing, 1974, p. 184). The government's record in extricating Britain from the increasingly hopeless obligations of the Palestine mandate and from imperial entrenchment in the Indian sub-continent should not obscure Bevin's determination to maintain Britain's power and influence in many other parts of the world, including the Eastern Mediterranean and the Middle East. After the granting of independence to India, Bevin could still tell the Commons that 'His Majesty's Government do not accept the view . . . that we have ceased to be a great power, or the contention that we have ceased to play that role' (quoted in Sked and Cook, 1979, p. 69). Not surprisingly, defence expenditure remained at a high level throughout the life of the government. By 1951 Britain was even committed to a higher *per capita* defence expenditure than the United States (Morgan, 1984, p. 279).

Labour's convictions about Britain's great power status determined its attitude towards two other major questions of overseas policy, the future of the Empire and the first tentative steps towards European integration. The granting of independence to India in 1947 was, of course, the most important element of Labour's imperial policy. Churchill's opposition to this move is well known and it would be wrong to deny all party differences on this question. But it had been the Conservative-dominated National Government which had passed the Government of India Act in 1935, which had clearly envisaged a transition to dominion status. Churchill's stance should not be taken as typical of the Conservative Party as a whole. When Labour's bill came up for its second reading on 10 July 1947, Churchill absented himself from the House and the Opposition's objections were presented in moderate terms by Harold Macmillan. As far as the rest of the Empire was concerned, Labour made significant moves in the field of colonial development, particularly in Nigeria and the Gold Coast, but there was no headlong rush towards independence. Britain would remain an imperial power into the forseeable future. Hugh Dalton once described the colonies as 'pullulating, poverty-stricken, diseased nigger communities' (Morgan, 1984, p. 194). In Malaya Labour embarked upon a military confrontation to root out Communist infiltration, a process which would continue throughout the 1950s. What is striking, however, is the degree to which the whole colonial question transcended party divisions. In 1945 Geoge Hall, Labour's Colonial Secretary, thanked his Conservative predecessor for laying the foundations of his own policy, and such bipartisan sentiments were to be reiterated by Oliver Lyttelton in the Conservative Government of 1951.

Bevin and the Labour Government as a whole adopted an extremely cool attitude towards the first signs of a European federalist movement in the late 1940s. Bevin's primary interest lay in securing adequate defence arrangements. This meant committing the United States to defend the European continent, and he was far more interested in developing Britain's links with the United States than in fostering European co-operation. In any case, with its shattered economy Europe at this time scarcely looked like an inviting partner for the British government, and when in 1950 the Schuman Plan proposed a pooling of sovereignty over the coal and steel industries of Western Europe, Labour held aloof. With Churchill and other leading Conservatives such as Macmillan and David Maxwell Fyfe apparently enthusiastic supporters of closer European integration, this did seem to be an area where the consensus did not run. Later events, however, would show that a Conservative government was no more interested than Labour in the development of a united Europe.

If the establishment of a postwar consensus is viewed as a movement by the two leading parties towards a common centre ground, that process was clearly not complete by 1945 in the case of the Conservatives. Indeed, in so far as there existed a core of policies common to the two parties by the end of the war, the electorate clearly did not fully believe in the Conservatives' commitment to it. Historians who have questioned the extent to which the war itself created a two-party consensus point to the importance of the immediate postwar years for the development of Conservative thinking. According to Kevin Jefferys, for example, 'the profound shock of Labour's overwhelming victory was ... to be of greater importance than the experience of war in shifting the Conservative party towards a fundamental reassessment of its domestic policy' (Jefferys, 1987b, p. 144; Eatwell, 1979, p. 159). Similarly Samuel Beer asserts that by 1945 Conservatism had not made a full or definite commitment to either the Welfare State or the managed economy (Beer, 1965, p. 308).

If for no other reason than Labour's electoral success in 1945, the Conservatives had no alternative but to integrate some of Labour's thinking into their own programme more clearly than they had yet managed to do. As Butler put it, 'until the progressive features of our thought had been fully exposed to public view, no one was going to kill Attlee in order to make Churchill king' (Butler, 1971, p. 132). Quintin Hogg thought the time was ripe for promulgating a new Tamworth Manifesto. This would necessitate asserting the ascendancy of the younger progressive elements in the party over the traditional libertarian strain. It was unlikely that the septuagenarian Churchill would play a major role in this process and in fact it was only the insistence of the 1946 Party Conference for a clear statement of what the party stood for that overrode his reluctance to authorize work on policy re-examination. Fortunately, as Leader of the Opposition, Churchill largely limited himself to making speeches on matters of foreign and defence policy. Furthermore, one of the beneficial effects of electoral defeat in 1945 and the loss of 173 seats was to clear out a large amount of parliamentary dead wood at a single stroke. The average age of the parliamentary party in 1945 was only 41 and the election of 1950 saw the recruitment of a large number of talented MPs who would set the tone of Conservatism in the 1950s and 1960s. The formation that year of the 'One Nation' group of younger MPs interested in progressive social legislation was symbolic of the change.

The leading figure in the reformulation of Conservative thinking was R. A. Butler, aided by the bright young men who, under his direction, staffed the revitalized Conservative Research Department, which became a think-tank of new ideas. From this fertile source there flowed a stream of new policy initiatives, which gradually transformed the party's tarnished image, enabling it to recapture much of the centre ground in the ongoing battle of ideas. In an important speech in March 1946 Butler called for a total reorganization of the social structure on which the party rested, an acceptance of redistributive taxation and a repudiation of *laissez-faire* economics. The *Manchester Guardian* commented that such goals would have the support of the majority of the Parliamentary Labour Party, while from the Conservative right Brendan Bracken wrote scathingly of 'neo-Socialists' who favoured nationalizing railways, electricity, gas and many other things (Horne, 1988, p. 299).

The publication of the *Industrial Charter* in 1947 was perhaps the nearest thing to the new Tamworth Manifesto for which Hogg had called. Butler saw the need to counter the charge that Conservatives were the party of industrial free-for-all. The Charter was therefore first and foremost an assurance that modern Conservatism would maintain a strong central guidance over the management of the economy in the interests of efficiency and full employment (R. A. Butler, 1971, p. 146). It accepted the nationalization of the mines, railways and Bank of England and spoke of new machinery for economic planning and fixing wages. But more important than the Charter's details — many of which were in fact dropped when the Tories returned to power — was the general impression that the Conservatives were moving towards the centre ground of benevolent inter-ventionism already occupied by Labour. The *Manchester Guardian* even wrote of 'Tory Socialism'. The Charter was accepted by the Party Conference in 1947 when Eden, reminding the delegates of their tradition of social reform, declared that Conservatives were not a 'party of unbridled, brutal capitalism'. It was followed in 1948 by the less important *Agricultural Charter* which basically accepted the interventionism of the government's Agriculture Act of 1947 with guaranteed price support for farmers. The Tory manifesto of 1950 was based on the Research Department's *The Right Road for Britain*, which had been published in July 1949. It seemed to differ from Labour's only in so far as it still stressed the importance of personal initiative and promised to return road transport and steel to the private sector. Butler and the Research Department had thus completed the transformation of the Conservative Party from its prewar stance to one that was both interventionist and forward-looking.

The Labour Party went into the General Election of 1950 with a new shopping list of industries to be nationalized, but one which would only have brought a further 500,000 workers into the public sector. Morrison had been careful to stress the empirical nature of the new programme at the Party Conference that year, and, as Labour's chief electoral strategist, sought to commit the party to a policy based on consolidation rather than innovation in order to retain the middle-class vote which Labour had been so successful in winning in 1945. In fact little was made of the party's nationalization plans in the campaign itself. The Tories too, committed now to the Welfare State and the mixed economy, presented themselves as a party of moderation, while trying to portray their opponents as class warriors. The practical effect, therefore, was that the party battalions fought their battles over a remarkably narrow field of conflict. Moderation seemed to be the order of the day. Harold Macmillan noted the way in which both parties had tended to move towards the middle ground. All but a few of the extreme left of the Labour Party were beaten; only three Communist candidates retained their deposits (Horne, 1988, p. 318).

Labour survived the election but with its massive overall majority of 1945 now reduced to a mere five seats. The closeness of the result, presaging an early return to the polls, and the feeling that Labour had lost its mandate, rather than any fundamental policy differences, made the new Parliament tense and acrimonious. But there were few further advances along the paths of socialism. Labour's shopping list of industries was quietly dropped; the *Daily Express* described Gaitskell's 1951 budget as a truly Tory measure.

Beset by death, illness and resignation among his senior ministers, Attlee went to the country again in October 1951. The party's manifesto was even more moderate than in 1950. It did not even contain the word socialism. There was no shopping list for nationalization, but only a vague promise to take into public ownership certain unspecified industries which were 'failing the nation'. The two major parties were increasingly trying to appeal to the same interests and emotions in the electorate. Of course, politicians did their best to emphasize points of party difference by exaggerating the position of their opponents. For Labour, Michael Foot warned against 'the mass unemployment which we always have under the Tories', while the Labour candidate for Bridgwater predicted that a Conservative government would mean wars all over the globe. Even Morrison accused Churchill of being a warmonger, a cry that was taken up in menacing tones by the *Daily Mirror*. But after six years of Labour government, much of it characterized by Crippsian austerity, the country was ready for a change. With an overall majority of 17 seats (though Labour still held the advantage in terms of the popular vote), the Conservatives with Churchill at their head returned to power. The reality of the consensus would now be put to the test.

3

The Consensus Confirmed,
1951–70

Labour built its 1951 election campaign around the fear that a Conservative victory would result in divisive domestic policies and aggressive and dangerous policies abroad. There were predictions of the dismantling of the Welfare State, conflict with the trade unions, renewed militarism and an end to colonial development. In fact none of these predictions was borne out by events. The historian of Churchill's postwar administration concludes that 'one of the most remarkable features of the Government was the extent that Conservative policy followed on logically from Labour policy in the preceding six years' (Seldon, 1981, p. 421). In his first parliamentary speech on returning to the premiership Churchill announced prophetically: 'Controversy there must be on some of the issues before us, but this will be a small part of the work and interests we have in common.' After they had been consolidated in power with an increased majority by the 1955 election, Attlee told the Durham Miners' Gala that the Conservatives owed their victory to their appropriation of Labour's policies: 'They have had to accept what we have done – many things which 20, 30 or 40 years ago they would have denounced as heresies and silly socialism' (Harris, 1982, p. 534). The consensus in fact was confirmed.

An important factor was the type of Conservative who now dominated the party. The government, of course, was headed by Winston Churchill, anxious to rid the party of its 1930s image. But at seventy-seven years of age the Prime Minister did little more than set the framework as far as domestic politics were concerned, reserving his failing energies for foreign and defence matters. The dominant voices of the new Conservatism throughout the 1950s were those of R. A. Butler, Harold Macmillan and, notwithstanding his immersion in questions of diplomacy, Anthony Eden. Despite the sometimes bitter personal rivalries between these three men, in terms of political philosophy there was little to separate them. Butler, of course, had already done much to establish his credentials as a consensus politician on the left of the party. Macmillan had been deeply affected by prewar unemployment in his con- stituency of Stockton-on-Tees. An early convert to Keynesianism before that economic philosophy had gained widespread acceptance, he never permitted his colleagues to forget their commitment to full employment. On becoming Conservative leader in 1957 Macmillan pronounced, in the best tradition of Disraeli's 'One Nation', that 'we have never been, and I trust that while I am your leader, we never will be, a party of any class or sectional interest' (Horne, 1989, p. 17). Eden's biographer has written: 'I always found his brand of humane, liberal and progressive Conservatism, born in the trenches on the Western Front in 1916, the only version that appealed to me' (James, 1986, p. xi). Indeed, during the war Eden had toyed with the idea of forming a new centrist coalition headed by Ernest Bevin and himself, or trying to construct a progressive Tory party with the help of younger men such as Butler.

Churchill, anxious to preserve domestic peace to pave the way for a last effort on his part to pull the world back from the brink of thermonuclear disaster, ensured that men such as these would set the tone of his government. The momentum of events since 1945 and the ongoing aspirations of the British people probably left him little choice. Churchill appointed Butler (rather than Oliver Lyttelton) to the Exchequer; Eden returned, almost inevitably, to the Foreign Office, universally recognized as heir-in-waiting for the premiership; and

Macmillan went to the Ministry of Housing, a post which assumed political prominence in view of the party's commitment to build 300,000 houses in a single year. Another important appointment was that of the emollient Walter Monckton as Minister of Labour. Maxwell Fyfe, whom many had expected to get the job, had ruffled feathers by hinting at the possibility of trade union legislation from a future Conservative government. From Labour's benches Richard Crossman judged that the new Conservative Cabinet was 'only very slightly to the right of the most recent Attlee Cabinet' (Crossman, 1981, p. 30).

The new government's economic policy was central to its overall strategy and a critical element in the consolidation of the consensus. Lord Croham, a future Head of the Treasury, believed that there was less change in 1951 than between any two governments in the whole postwar era (Hennessy and Seldon, 1987, p. 79). Certainly the new government stopped short of restoring the full-blooded capitalist economy which critics had anticipated and which would have pleased some backbench Tories such as Ralph Assheton, the powerful chairman of the party's Finance Committee. In fact it almost immediately introduced an Excess Profits Tax. A Treasury plan, code-named 'Robot', which would have allowed the pound to float and involved abandoning the commitment to full employment, was put forward in the spring of 1952, but such free-market adventures were quickly abandoned. Calls to 'set the people free' proved to be little more than rhetoric, while the government even recognized the need to continue the rationing of basic foods for the time being. Eventually they were able to continue the trend begun by Harold Wilson with his 'bonfire of controls' in 1948.

Early in 1954 *The Economist* invented the mythical composite personality of Mr Butskell, a combination of the names of Butler and his Labour predecessor, Hugh Gaitskell (*The Economist*, 13 February 1954). Ever since, the hybrid concept of Butskellism has epitomized the consensus, particularly in its economic aspects. The economist Samuel Brittan has described it as 'an interesting mixture of planning and freedom, based on the economic teachings of Lord Keynes' (Brittan, 1964, p. 162). Yet some historians have disputed the extent of continuity between Gaitskell and Butler. Keith Middlemas, for example, points to the revival of interest in monetary policy and the reduction of planning under Butler (Middlemas, 1986, p. 269). Gaitskell, as his biographer shows, objected to the term 'Butskellism' as a 'silly catchword', and claimed that he was much more willing than Butler to use the budget as an instrument of economic control. Certainly the two men had different long-term visions of the distribution of wealth (Williams, 1979, p. 313). But such criticisms are a counsel of perfection in the analysis of a fundamental consensus. The general pattern remained a basic commitment to the mixed economy and Keynesian budgetary planning and demand management. Butler was anxious to show that the Conservatives were not the party of unemployment, and resisted calls from some of his colleagues for drastic cuts in public expenditure. Though Gaitskell may not have felt flattered to be so closely linked with a Conservative, contemporaries cannot have been entirely mistaken in their perceptions. It is worth noting the reported reaction of the Conservative MP, Robert Boothby, to Butler's appointment in October 1951. More than two years before *The Economist* coined 'Butskellism', he is said to have remarked, 'Why that's Gaitskell all over again, but from Cambridge' (Crossman, 1981, p. 30). Butler himself conceded that he and Gaitskell both spoke the language of Keynesianism, albeit 'with different accents and with a differing emphasis' (R. A. Butler, 1971, p. 160). Importantly, after a difficult beginning as a result of the Korean War, Butler's stewardship proved reasonably successful. It was a time when world factors were more generally favourable to the British economy than in any subsequent period. Butler's years as Chancellor thus came to be seen as a model for future practice by governments of both political complexions.

The new government's attitude towards its inheritance of state-owned industry provided an important test of the reality of the consensus. Experience proved that nationalization was an element of the consensus where rhetoric and practice were widely separated. Churchill's government confirmed those boundaries between the public and private sectors which survived largely intact for the next three decades. The Conservatives denationalized only the steel and road haulage industries. In the case of steel, Labour's plans had not yet progressed very far, nationalization only having come into effect in January 1951, so the process of denationalization was relatively straightforward. In any case the government preserved a large measure of central control through the Iron and Steel Board, despite the preference of some ministers such as Harry Crookshank and Lord Woolton for a more radical approach. The Conservative bill caused little controversy, though Labour went through the ritual of opposition. At one time debate was adjourned as less than 40 MPs were present (Seldon, 1981, p. 191). The Transport Bill proved more contentious, but in the end road haulage was only partially returned to the private sector because of the difficulty of finding buyers. Denationalization went no further. Churchill stressed: 'It is only where we believed that a measure of nationalisation was a real hindrance to our island life that we have reversed the policy' (quoted in Seldon, 1981, p. 187). Nationalization had almost been stripped of its ideological content.

In the elections of 1950 and 1951 Labour had predicted that a Conservative victory would mean drastic cutbacks in the social services. In his first budget Butler did introduce some health service charges, but Gaitskell himself had been the first Chancellor to breach the principle of a free health service in his budget of 1951. Thereafter, however, as the economy strengthened, the Conservatives actually increased spending on the social services, taking satisfaction in proclaiming their virtue in this respect. The broad fabric of the Welfare State was maintained, even enhanced. In December 1951 the Cabinet's Economy Committee dropped plans for hospital charges. It was a sign that attacks on the Welfare State were politically unacceptable. Successive Conservative Ministers of Health in the 1950s buried the notion that Tories were out to destroy the National Health Service. The Guillebaud Committee reported in 1953 that the Health Service was providing value for money and the government accepted its conclusions. 'It is difficult to imagine', concludes Anthony Seldon, 'that Labour would have managed the N.H.S. very differently in these years' (Seldon, 1981, p. 270).

It is, of course, the Labour Party with which the trade union movement traditionally enjoys a close and intimate relationship, yet during Churchill's government the unions were brought closer to a Conservative administration than for many years past. Churchill, with his role during the General Strike not forgotten, was keen to pursue a policy of industrial appeasement, even if this meant inflationary wage settlements. He was determined, wrote Woolton, that there should be few industrial strikes during his period as Prime Minister (Woolton, 1959, pp. 379–80). Sir Walter Monckton, the new Minister of Labour, was predisposed towards conciliation and all his energies were devoted to bringing the two sides of industry together. Monckton's typical reaction to an industrial dispute was to set up an inquiry to enforce a compromise. At the last moment, however, under instructions from the Prime Minister, he was always ready to give the unions what they demanded rather than weaken the corporate structure that had been created during and after the war. It was an astonishing commentary on this period that Arthur Deakin, General Secretary of the Transport and General Workers' Union, could say in 1953, 'I believe Sir Walter Monckton has given us a square deal and we have been able to do things that were difficult to do under our own people' (quoted in Seldon, 1981, p. 202).

Anthony Seldon has shown that across the range of domestic ministries, from fuel and power to pensions via agriculture, the degree of genuine inter-party disagreement was kept to a minimum and the consensus maintained. Though Labour made education policy an area of vigorous debate, *The Times* could still comment in April 1953 that there was little to divide the two parties. Debate was beginning on the value of comprehensive schools, but this had not yet become a serious issue of inter-party dispute. Much the same picture emerges from an examination of the government's overseas policy. None of Labour's dire predictions proved correct, at least until the Suez disaster of 1956. Labour backbenchers, particularly those on the left, found plenty to criticize, but as far as the party leadership was concerned, disagreements were rare and 'mainly on questions of priorities' (Seldon, 1981, p. 415). Eden could justly tell the Party Conference in 1954: 'I always believe that the more bipartisan our foreign policy can be, the stronger the authority of the Foreign Secretary of the day' (quoted in Seldon, 1981, p. 414).

Far from intensifying the Cold War, Churchill laboured mightily, if vainly, to bring the great powers together at a summit conference. More fruitfully, Eden as Foreign Secretary achieved a string of diplomatic triumphs, not least his skilful handling of the Geneva Conference on Indochina in 1954. The Conservatives, of course, had no difficulty in maintaining the basis of Labour's foreign policy − a close partnership with the United States in a still tense and dangerous world. In the first defence debate in the Commons after the 1951 election, Churchill paid tribute to the outgoing Labour Government 'for several most important decisions about our defence policy which ... form the foundation on which we stand today' (quoted in Seldon, 1981, p. 15). Critically, the Conservatives continued Labour's policy of giving priority to the RAF and building up a nuclear bomber force as the basis of the country's frontline defence.

The foreign policy consensus appeared to break down in a most spectacular fashion in 1956, after Eden had succeeded to the premiership. The occasion was the famous Suez Crisis when Britain, in conjunction with France and in collusion with Israel, invaded Egypt in response to Colonel Nasser's nationalization of the Suez Canal Company. The government's actions were roundly condemned by the overwhelming majority of world opinion and there was no doubting the sincerity of the vehement opposition coming from the Labour Party. For many the normal courtesies of cross-party behaviour became for a while impossible. Yet it is important to stress that Labour's fury was directed at the way in which Eden tried to recover the Canal rather than the government's underlying case. In its initial reaction Labour had been at one with the Conservatives in condemning Nasser's action. Gaitskell described it as 'high-handed and totally unjustified', while another Labour MP, Reginald Paget, spoke of the perils of appeasing dictators (James, 1986, pp. 455–6). It was the government's well-concealed resort to force, at a time when many still hoped for a peaceful settlement through the United Nations, together with the first hints of collusion with Israel, which fractured the bipartisan response to Nasser's aggression.

Policy towards Europe provides one of the most interesting, and even surprising, illustrations of the consensus. By his stirring speeches in the late 1940s Churchill had put himself at the head of the movement for a more united Europe, and enthusiasts expected great things from him when the Conservatives returned to power after the cool response of the Labour Government. But Churchill's rhetoric had not been analysed as closely as it should have been. It is doubtful whether he ever envisaged sinking British sovereignty within a federal Europe. Pro-Europeans in the cabinet, such as Macmillan and Maxwell Fyfe, found their high hopes quickly dashed by Churchill and Eden. At a press conference shortly after taking office, Eden made it perfectly clear that the new government had no more intention of joining the European Defence Community than had its predecessor. Thus the pattern was set which would see the countries of Western Europe, with Britain excluded, move towards the creation of the Common Market with the signing of the Treaty of Rome in 1957.

Commonwealth and colonial policy showed how far the Conservative Party of the 1950s had moved on from its prewar traditions. There were still right-wing imperialists holding high office – Lord Salisbury even became Commonwealth Secretary in 1952 – but it was not they who set the tone of the government's policy. Even Churchill, himself a product of the age of Victorian imperialism, bowed to the inevitable. The inexorable progress of the colonial territories towards independence was not really a contentious issue in these years, however much Labour tried to make it such. The Opposition's fury was largely a sham. Kavanagh and Morris conclude that it was in the area of colonial policy 'that post-war bipartisanship was perhaps at its strongest' (Kavanagh and Morris, 1989, p. 97). Oliver Lyttelton, appointed Colonial Secretary in 1951, was the first of a series of liberal-minded ministers, culminating with Iain Macleod in 1959, who oversaw the process by which the old Empire was transformed into a multiracial Commonwealth. By Macleod's time the rush towards decolonization was becoming almost a stampede, with the government now willing to concede independence well in advance of being forced to do so.

By the mid-1950s, therefore, the consensus had become a centrepiece of British political life. It was perhaps no coincidence that in 1953 Edw d Hyams wrote a novel entitled *Gentian Violet* in which . leading character succeeded in getting elected to Parliament both as a Conservative and as a socialist without being found out. After another Conservative election victory in 1955, Parliament reassembled to debate the Queen's Speech of a government now headed by Eden. After Attlee had spoken, the Prime Minister could 'only thank him' for his words. His speech 'was so kind and so gentle and so generally approving that I feel we can go forward with the execution of this formidable programme under the benevolent aegis of the Honourable Members opposite' (quoted in Harris, 1982, p. 536). Across a wide range of policies the Conservatives had pursued and continued to pursue a broad line of continuity from their Labour predecessors. There had been few sharp reversals. Indeed, the Tories had tended to accelerate trends already marked out by Labour. The era of change and reorganization inaugurated by the wartime coalition was at an end and the Conservatives had no intention of reversing what had been accomplished since 1940. There had been no second watershed despite the change of government in 1951. According to Paul Addison, 'in their different ways the two main parties [now] lacked ideological purpose' (Addison, 1985, p. 198).

For Labour these years were marked, as so often when the party is out of power, by division and internecine strife. The beginnings of a left-wing revolt against the leadership had been seen while Labour was still in power, when Bevan, Wilson

49

and John Freeman resigned from the government after Gaitskell introduced charges for false teeth and spectacles in 1951. During the 1950s the left had its moments of triumph. In Parliament it often took the lead, since the party hierarchy found little in the Conservatives' policies to which it took serious exception. 'The vacuum of opposition was therefore filled by left-wing noise' (Sked and Cook, 1979, p. 136). In particular, the Bevanites rejected Attlee's continuing bipartisanship and clamoured for an alternative, socialist foreign policy. At the 1952 Party Conference the left all but swept the board in the constituency party section of elections to the National Executive Committee. In 1953 Labour adopted a policy document, 'Challenge to Britain', which promised a further dose of nationalization. It also promised an extension of comprehensive education and the phasing out of all private schools, together with the abolition of health service charges. In the main, however, the right wing kept its hands firmly on the reins of power.

The critical development was the leadership battle which ensued when Attlee finally decided to retire after the General Election of 1955. Gaitskell's comprehensive victory over Morrison and Bevan ensured that, perhaps more clearly than at any time in its history, Labour would compete with the Tories for the centre ground of British politics. For Gaitskell was far less concerned than Attlee had been to use the leadership to unite the disparate factions that make up the British Labour Party. He never sought to conceal his own position on the party's intellectual right or his contempt for its Marxist fringe. As one left-wing critic bemoaned, the Gaitskellites 'saw Labour achieving power and retaining it only through a more efficient, technological management of a capitalist society' (Duff, 1971, p. 77). Of equal importance was the clear ascendancy of the revisionist right in the intellectual battles of the 1950s. While the left seemed bankrupt of new ideas, the right produced an impressive flow of fresh thinking. Of seminal importance was Anthony Crosland's *The Future of Socialism*, published in 1956. Crosland argued that socialism was about equality rather than public ownership. If that was true, nationalization could be

50

relegated to the status of a redundant instrument in the achievement of a socialist state. Keynesian economics would be sufficient to secure Labour's goals.

Gaitskell did have plenty of trouble from Labour's left, particularly after the party's third successive electoral defeat in 1959. His battles to remove Clause Four from the party's constitution — 'we have ... long ago come to accept ... a mixed economy' — and to stave off a conference commitment to unilateral nuclear disarmament gave advance warning of the growing power of the left that would one day confront his successor. But the party bequeathed to Harold Wilson's leadership following Gaitskell's premature death in 1963 was firmly anchored in the centre ground of British politics, notwithstanding Wilson's earlier dalliance on the Bevanite left. Labour was a realistic contender for power once more.

The Conservatives were in power for thirteen years between 1951 and 1964. The period saw four different Prime Ministers, Churchill (1951—5), Eden (1955—7), Macmillan (1957—63) and Douglas-Home (1963—4), but there was an essential continuity of policies. During this time the party won three successive general elections (1951, 1955 and 1959), increasing its majority on each occasion, and leading some political commentators to conclude that the Labour Party was in long-term and irreversible decline, with little prospect of again forming a government. Such a pattern might suggest that the electorate, on being offered a clear choice between Conservative and Labour alternatives, decisively endorsed the former and rejected the latter. The reality, however, was somewhat different. Interestingly, before the 1959 campaign took place, a public opinion poll revealed that almost 40 per cent of voters believed that it made no difference which party was in power. The Conservatives were fortunate to hold office at a time of visible affluence. It was a period of conspicuous consumption after the austerity and deprivation of the war years and the immediate postwar era. More and more people were able to afford the trappings of what had previously been thought of as a middle-class lifestyle — home ownership, annual holidays, televisions, washing machines and the like. It was a society well characterized by Macmillan's famous 'never had it so good' remark made at Bedford in 1957. Later critics argued that the nation's wealth was misdirected during the 1950s at the expense of the long-term reconstruction and development of British industry. But some sort of material pay-off for the generation which had grown up in the 1930s and then fought the war was probably a political necessity by this time, whichever party had been in power.

The country was sufficiently contented with its growing prosperity to re-elect the Tories twice. The marginal voter, who determines the outcome of British elections, was happy to see a party which seemed to exude competence carry on. This is a far more realistic explanation of the electoral history of the 1950s than the idea that the country was emphatically rejecting a markedly different set of options on offer from Labour. There seemed no good reason to change a winning team, particularly when Labour's image was damaged by its own internal disputes and bickering. In reality the major improvements in the British economy during this period would probably have occurred irrespective of any policy decisions made by the government. World factors were decisive. The government enjoyed a windfall from two significant changes in the terms of trade. After the end of the Korean War, food and raw material prices fell so dramatically that in 1953 the country could buy 13 per cent more imports than in 1951 for the same amount of exports. A minor world recession in 1957—8 triggered off another, slower slump in commodity prices. Thus the country, along with the industrialized West as a whole, enjoyed a long boom, favourable both to full employment and an expansion of the social services. Perhaps the Conservatives' most significant contribution to the country's economic well-being was to allow the burden of defence spending to fall as a result of increasing reliance on the nuclear deterrent rather than conventional forces. This was the main reason why taxation fell as a proportion of national income for several years running.

Eden's government was overshadowed by foreign policy and especially the Suez Crisis. So has been, thus far, its examination by historians, but Richard Lamb has shown how, on the domestic front, Eden was determined to preserve the harmony of the two front benches. Wage-push inflation was showing signs of becoming a serious problem and some economic commentators called for cuts in public spending and a rise in the number out of work. The City felt that a showdown with the trade unions was essential if the wage-price spiral was to be broken, and Lamb concludes that a great opportunity was missed in 1955 for trade union reform, since the moderate union leaders of that time would probably have accepted government measures without too much opposition (Lamb, 1987, pp. 14, 28).

Eden's successor, Macmillan, was even more determined that there should be no return to deflationary policies and pre-Keynesian economics. As he wrote in his memoirs, 'encouraged by my old friend, Roy Harrod [biographer of Keynes], I still resisted the idea of deflation as a permanent or even prolonged policy' (Macmillan, 1971, p. 355). But Macmillan's premiership did witness a significant challenge to a central tenet of the postwar consensus, even though it came from within the ranks of his own party rather than the Labour benches opposite. The Prime Minister's first Chancellor, Peter Thorneycroft, soon became concerned at the ever-rising level of government expenditure and the growing risk of inflation. In 1957 he announced his determination to maintain the parity of the pound even if this meant higher unemployment, and before the end of the year he was talking of holding government expenditure at its existing level. The postwar objectives of full employment and economic expansion seemed to be on the brink of being abandoned. But in 1958, when Macmillan refused to endorse a package of spending cuts, Thorneycroft resigned, taking with him his two junior ministers, Nigel Birch and Enoch Powell.

It is now clear that the debate did not end with Thorneycroft's resignation. His two successors, Derick Heathcoat Amory and Selwyn Lloyd, shared his concern over inflation. Amory later recalled a most revealing conversation he had had with the Prime Minister. '"What is wrong with inflation,

Derry!" I'd reply, "You're thinking of your constituency in the 1930s?" — "Yes, I'm thinking of the under-use of resources — let's over-use them!"' (quoted in Horne, 1989, p. 140). But despite mounting evidence that inflation was a genuine problem, Macmillan set his face against any suggestion of prolonged deflation. According to Lloyd, the Prime Minister's greatest mistake was 'thinking unemployment a worse enemy than uncontrolled inflation' (quoted in Thorpe, 1989, p. 360). When in 1962 Lloyd, together with a third of the Cabinet, was sacked in Macmillan's famous 'Night of the Long Knives', Nigel Birch wrote cuttingly to *The Times* that 'for the second time the Prime Minister has got rid of a Chancellor of the Exchequer who tried to get expenditure under control'. The dispute was basically between those who, like Macmillan, were still haunted by memories of the 1930s, and who firmly held that increased state spending was needed to build a happy and united nation, and those who viewed such a strategy as likely ultimately to lead to economic disaster.

Such debates within the Conservative Party caused little more than a ripple on the surface of cross-party consensus. Indeed, after the 1959 General Election, that consensus appeared to be moving leftwards again. In the early 1960s the parties competed with one another in their ability to create faster economic growth and then distribute the fruits of that growth. Public spending plans actually grew on the assumption that higher rates of growth could be achieved in the future. Growth became an economic panacea. It would enable the government to spend more on social welfare, while protecting workers' take-home pay. Whereas Conservative rhetoric since 1951 had been permeated with slogans about freedom, Macmillan and Lloyd now seemed ready to achieve growth through planning and controls. With the setting up of the National Economic Development Council (1961) and the National Incomes Commission (1962), and the introduction of an incomes policy, Conservatism moved nearer to embracing a corporate state and *dirigiste* society than ever before or since. The NEDC ('Neddy') was particularly important in representing an attempt to bring government, unions and management together to plan the future of British industry and promote economic growth for the benefit of all. Whereas such planning had hitherto been associated with Labour, the initiative now came from Macmillan and Lloyd, supported by the Federation of British Industries.

Notwithstanding these policy initiatives, the Conservative Party rapidly lost its political momentum from 1962 onwards. Above all the government, and particularly the Prime Minister, lost their reputations for competence which had been so important in winning electoral endorsement during the 1950s. Sustained growth proved unattainable without dangerously overheating the economy. Labour derided the government's economic management as the era of 'stop-go'. A succession of policy reverses — de Gaulle's veto on Britain's application to join the European Economic Community in 1963 was perhaps the most significant — was compounded by a series of spy and sex scandals. In the most notorious, John Profumo, Minister of War, resigned after admitting an affair with a prostitute who had also shared her bed with a Russian diplomat. There was a widespread feeling that the Conservatives had been in power too long. Labour would make great play in the 1964 election with the slogan, 'Thirteen Wasted Years'. Macmillan, whose calm imperturbability and patrician demeanour had once been great assets, now suddenly appeared old and out of touch. In the growing cult of youth, epitomized in the new American President, John F. Kennedy, the Prime Minister seemed an anachronism. Labour was clearly making considerable progress with what might be called the intellectual voter — perhaps for the first time since 1945. The press and the media were becoming vocal critics of the Conservative Government. Even the BBC — for long regarded as a friend of the conservative establishment — emerged in a new role, presenting such satirical programmes as *That Was the Week that Was*. The Conservatives' eclipse in the early 1960s was thus as much cultural as political. This situation was skilfully exploited by a revived Labour Party, and particularly its new leader Harold Wilson. Though the Conservatives made a substantial recovery during the year of Alec Douglas-Home's premiership, it was not sufficient to prevent a Labour victory in 1964 by the narrow overall majority of five seats.

In that election voters were apparently offered a clear choice, if only between the former fourteenth earl, transposed reluctantly as Wilson suggested from a Scottish grousemoor, and the Labour leader with his North Country accent and exaggeratedly working-class credentials. Yet in policy terms the choice was less clear-cut. According to David Robertson the election manifestos of the two parties were closer together on the central issue of economic policy than at any time in the previous forty years (Robertson, 1976, p. 98). Labour probably won in 1964 on the successful projection of an image rather than an alternative set of policies. Iain Macleod's analysis of the Conservative defeat is instructive: 'For the first time in five elections our grip on the centre has weakened' (Fisher, 1973, p. 259).

As usually happens when Labour takes office, there were expectations in some quarters that the victory of 1964 would mean a distinct advance towards a socialist society. 'We began to feel that the Left was on its way,' recorded Barbara Castle (1984, p. ix). Indeed it was part of Wilson's success as party leader that he was able largely to satisfy his own left wing, some of whom fondly believed that one of their own number now occupied 10 Downing Street. But Wilson was an inherently cautious premier. He proved stronger on rhetoric than genuine ideological conviction. 'Socialism, as I understand it,' he said in 1963, 'means applying a sense of purpose to our national life: economic purpose, social purpose and moral purpose. Purpose means technical skill' (quoted in Kavanagh, 1987, p. 158). If Wilson had ever been truly of the party's left wing, he had moved considerably towards the right since his Bevanite days. His administration proved to be 'a cautious, conservative, tentative Government, deeply suspicious of truly radical departures' (James, 1972, p. 81). The new Prime Minister was not reluctant to make symbolic gestures. Prescription charges were abolished and well-known left-wingers, Barbara Castle and Jennie Lee (widow of Aneurin Bevan), were appointed to the new ministries of Overseas Development and the Arts. Neither, of course, was in a position to advance socialism. Even the new Department of Economic Affairs, headed by George Brown and championing the much heralded National Plan, achieved little and lost much of its authority after 1966. The only measure of nationalization promised in the party's manifesto was the renationalization of steel. 'Of any intention of creating a socialist Britain . . . the 1964 government was entirely innocent' (Campbell, 1987, p. 374). Not surprisingly, there was soon talk of a realignment of Liberal and Labour parties in a non-socialist, moderate, reforming movement of the left. Little changed when Labour sought, and received, a clearer electoral mandate in 1966. Apart from steel renationalization, which had not been achieved in the 1964–6 Parliament because of the fragility of the government's majority, there was little mention of socialism. Despite public apathy on the issue, Wilson knew that the steel pledge would help keep the left happy.

The rhetoric of inter-party animosity increased during the Wilson years, but this owed much to a personal antipathy between the Prime Minister and the new Conservative leader, Edward Heath, who succeeded Douglas-Home in 1965, and a growing disdain for Wilson as a political trickster on the Conservative benches as a whole. The 1970 Tory manifesto condemned Labour's 'cheap and trivial style of government'. In fact, 'Heath and Wilson shared far more objectives and assumptions than fundamental divides' (Whitehead, 1985, p. 50). By the time of the General Election of 1970 a *Punch* cartoon showed Wilson hanging on grimly to the coat-tails of Conservatism as he moved ever further away from socialism (D. Butler, 1989, p. 26).

In line with the trend of the Conservative Government's economic policy over the previous Parliament, Labour entered office in 1964 convinced that the solution to what was by then seen as a national economic malaise lay in faster growth and the modernization of managerial methods. In another of his celebrated phrases, Wilson spoke of the 'white-hot heat of technology'. Results, however, were disappointing. Over the period of Labour Government, 1964–70, the annual average rate of growth was only 2.2 per cent. What was striking,

57

however, was the way in which the government used methods and instruments which had their origins in the Macmillan and Home governments. 'Much of the small print of the 1965 National Plan and Mr. Wilson's own "purposive physical intervention" had already been enacted before Labour came to power' (Brittan, 1971, p. 290). The fundamental continuity was particularly evident after the sterling crisis of 1966. There were to be no seismic shifts in macro-economic policy.

Wilson's government failed to avoid the basic problem which had beset the Tories, particularly after the mid-1950s — that attempts to accelerate growth resulted in higher imports, a balance-of-payments deficit and a crisis of confidence in sterling, leading to a period of enforced restraint. In the context of the postwar consensus, Wilson and his Chancellors (James Callaghan, 1964–7, and Roy Jenkins, 1967–70) proved to be rigidly orthodox. During the crisis of 1966 the Cabinet, faced with a stark choice between deflation and devaluation, opted for a massive dose of the former. Like its Conservative predecessor, the Labour Government placed the defence of sterling and the balance of payments ahead of growth, a strategy which many now believe did lasting damage to the British economy. When devaluation was finally adopted in 1967, it was done as a last resort rather than a positive policy option. Though Jenkins did much to restore a sound economy, the cost was high in terms of increased taxation and expenditure cuts.

Governmental attitudes towards the trade unions showed an interesting development in the shape of the consensus during the Wilson years. Ever since they had acquired a new legitimacy during the national struggle against Hitler, the unions had been treated with kid gloves and increasingly drawn into a shared responsibility for the management of the economy to defend full employment and promote economic expansion. Governments of both parties had shown a determination to work with rather than against the unions, a process which reached a climax with the creation of the NEDC under Selwyn Lloyd in 1961. From the late 1950s, however, the unions began to suffer a decline in popular esteem. They were thought to be too powerful and yet not able to control the actions of their own members, with the unofficial wildcat strike led by un-representative, militant, left-wing shop stewards becoming a particular bogy in the public mind. At all events, the unions' capacity for damage was thought to be excessive. Such feelings were encouraged by the succession of a new generation of union leaders such as Frank Cousins, Hugh Scanlon and Jack Jones, whose political views were decidedly to the left of those of their predecessors.

During the Wilson years the problem became acute. In the two years 1963—4 about four million working days were lost through strikes. In the two years 1968—9 the total had increased to about 11.5 million. The Labour Government itself believed that the damaging dock strike of 1967, which Wilson condemned as being politically inspired, was a major factor in making devaluation unavoidable. With the thinking of the Conservative Party moving in the same direction, it was in many ways a high point of the postwar consensus that it should have been a Labour Government, and more particularly the one-time Bevanite, Harold Wilson, and his new Employment Secretary, the left-winger, Barbara Castle, who determined in 1969 to introduce a legal framework into industrial relations. The government's proposals, embodied in the white paper *In Place of Strife*, were not a carbon copy of the Conservative document, *Fair Deal at Work*, but there were some striking similarities. It was a balanced package which would have given the trade unions considerable advantages in return for accepting certain binding obligations. But the unions themselves were outraged by the proposal, which would have enabled the Secretary of State to require those involved in a dispute to desist from strike action for up to 28 days. Vic Feather, General Secretary of the TUC, claimed that the suggested legislation would have introduced 'the taint of criminality' into industrial relations. Opposition was not confined to the trade unions themselves. Inside the Parliamentary Labour Party and within the Cabinet itself (with James Callaghan leading the rebels), objections mounted. Tony Benn, who had begun by supporting the proposals, recorded the change of mood: 'There is growing anxiety in the Cabinet, and I am now joining the anxious group, fearing that an Industrial Relations Bill just can't work' (Benn, 1988, p. 186). Eventually Wilson and Castle had to give way, and on 18 June 1969 accepted a face-saving formula in which the TUC General Council issued a 'solemn and binding undertaking' that its member unions would observe the TUC's own guidelines on unofficial strikes. As will be seen, this was an important date in the ultimate demise of the postwar consensus. Wilson had let go a unique opportunity to tip the balance of industrial relations marginally in favour of management in a way that could have had 'untold consequences for the future cost of labour and, through that, for all-round economic health' (Hennessy and Seldon, 1987, p. 199).

Not surprisingly, there was little open conflict between the major parties on foreign and defence policies between 1964 and 1970. Division was far more apparent within Labour's own ranks. Labour's course proved to be strikingly similar to that which would have been charted by a Conservative government. Labour's 1964 manifesto declared of the country's nuclear deterrent, whose retention had been a cardinal feature in the Conservative programme: 'It will not be independent and it will not be British and it will not deter.' Yet in office both the deterrent and loyalty to the United States remained cornerstones of Labour's foreign policy. Wilson even failed to distance himself significantly from America's growing involvement in the Vietnam War, much to the outrage of his own left wing. There were some minor reductions in British commitments. Some defence projects, such as the TSR 2 aircraft and a fifth Polaris submarine, were dropped, but overall little changed, with Britain maintaining a significant defence presence east of Suez. This was scarcely surprising for anyone who took note of Wilson's Mansion House speech in November 1964, in which the Prime Minister declared, 'We are a world power and a world influence or we are nothing.' This, commented the American correspondent Drew Middleton, 'sounds like any Tory statement' (quoted in Childs, 1986, p. 170). Two years later Wilson could still maintain that Britain's frontier was on the Himalayas. Only in 1968, and under the impact of compelling financial expediency rather than any socialist beliefs, did the government embark on a serious and wide-ranging reappraisal of the country's grossly over-extended defence liabilities, a process which led to the effective abandonment of any military role east of Suez.

The increasing hollowness of Britain's supposed status as a world power was one of the factors which persuaded Wilson to change course on the issue of Europe. At the time of Macmillan's abortive application for membership of the EEC, the Labour Party under Gaitskell had been divided but on balance hostile. Wilson, however, encouraged by such pro-Europeans in his cabinet as George Brown and Roy Jenkins, came to the conclusion that in a rapidly changing world Britain's future lay in Europe. The multiracial Commonwealth had long been a Labour ideal, and a possible alternative to closer integration with Europe. But the 1960s were a time of mounting disillusionment with the legacy of Britain's imperial past. As the newly independent members of the Commonwealth increasingly abandoned British ways and ideals, a rapid reappraisal took place in Labour's ranks. *Faute de mieux* a European future seemed the only option. Wilson's application in 1967 proved as futile as Macmillan's had been in the face of de Gaulle's steadfast and highly individualistic opposition to British membership. But its importance in the present context is that the consensus had been maintained, albeit somewhat precariously in view of the deep-seated misgivings on the Labour benches, and in very different terms from that which had existed on the European issue in the period 1945—57.

On the question of education the postwar consensus seemed likely to break down on the issue of selection for secondary schools. After 1966 the government went ahead with plans to implement a comprehensive scheme. The majority of Conservative MPs wanted a clear opposition to this policy and defence of the grammar schools, but it is noticeable that the Tory spokesman, Sir Edward Boyle, with Heath's support, was more guarded in his reaction. Though opposing compulsion, Boyle favoured the comprehensive principle and the ending of selection at the age of eleven. A considerable amount of progressive, some would say permissive, social legislation on issues such as capital punishment, abortion and homosexuality reached the statute book during the lifetime of Wilson's government. It was legislation which might well not have succeeded under a Conservative administration. But most of it derived from back bench initiatives rather than government proposals. On occasions the government behaved in a far less liberal fashion, as when, in 1968, it hurriedly passed restrictive immigration legislation when confronted with the prospect of a wave of East African Asians entering the country.

Not surprisingly, by the time that Wilson's government came to an end in 1970, the Labour left felt profoundly disillusioned. It was not only that the cause of socialism had not been advanced. With the management of the economy becoming ever more difficult, Labour had had to reintroduce prescription charges and increase charges for school meals. The building of new homes had declined, while the numbers out of work increased. The 'pragmatism' upon which Wilson had once placed great virtue seemed to have degenerated into a series of crisis expedients, devoid of any real strategy to cope with the growing problems of the national economy. On top of this were such 'Tory' measures as wage restraint, proposed curbs on trade unions, immigration controls and support for American 'imperialism' in Vietnam. Tony Benn recorded that it was during this period that 'my own radicalisation took shape, and I began ... to formulate policies which were more explicitly democratic and socialist' (Benn, 1988, p. xii). On the other hand, if Labour activists felt depressed, Conservatives could not even claim that Wilson had made a success of consensus politics. The great strength of the postwar consensus had been its apparent capacity to deliver continuing material prosperity. Now even that seemed to be in doubt. It was in these circumstances that Edward Heath entered Downing Street, pledged 'to change the course of history of this nation, nothing less'. After a quarter of a century it seemed that the consensus might be about to collapse.

4

The Consensus Challenged, 1970–79

The 1960s proved a disappointing decade as far as the performance of the British economy was concerned. It is scarcely surprising, therefore, that it was in this area that the postwar consensus first began to break down. In a revealing comment, Keith Joseph once remarked that 'the seeds of break in the consensus were being continuously implanted by disappointed expectations' (Joseph, 1987, p. 28). As has been seen, governments of both political parties had, since about 1947, pursued broadly Keynesian policies. The apparent problem by the 1960s was the inability of a Keynesian approach to produce growth, full employment *and* a stable level of prices. In restrospect it is not certain that all policies pursued since the establishment of the consensus had been truly Keynesian. After all, Keynes himself had died in 1946. His writings had prescribed remedies for the economic conditions of the 1930s and 1940s and it is by no means clear that he would have agreed with subsequent interpretations of his ideas as applied to the 1950s and 1960s. Almost certainly Keynes would have taken a more concerned view of the problem of inflation than did some of his later disciples.

Typically, economists who professed to be Keynesians were willing to risk price rises of around 2 or 3 per cent per annum in order to remove the danger of a deficiency of demand and therefore unemployment. Unfortunately, policies of economic expansion regularly resulted in a balance-of-payments deficit as imports were sucked into the country. This led in turn to pressure on the country's foreign currency reserves and on the exchange rate. Because politicians of both parties continually argued that 'sterling must have first priority', the response was then temporarily to deflate the economy in order to demonstrate prudent financial management to the international money markets. During Selwyn Lloyd's time as Chancellor this strategy achieved notoriety as the tactics of 'stop-go'. But previous Chancellors had experienced similar difficulties. Thorneycroft's resignation in 1958 has already been noted. Even earlier, Butler's 1955 budget had been an overtly electioneering measure. It had allowed the economy to get overheated, with the result that corrective measures were necessary once the election was out of the way. Many would now look to this time, reinforced by Monckton's concessions to the unions, as the moment when the inflationary wage spiral first began to get hold of the postwar economy (Horne, 1988, p. 378).

Contemporaries, however, took comfort in the belief that, with only a little pain, they could always bring the situation back under control. According to the so-called Phillips Curve, the government could trade off price stability against a slowdown in economic expansion. Minor adjustments in demand management would reduce inflation at the cost of a small rise in unemployment. Thus it was thought possible to manage the economy by choosing between different amounts of inflation and unemployment, depending on the situation at the time. But by the end of the Wilson Government it was clear that the British economy could experience rising inflation *and* rising unemployment at the same time. The term stagflation was coined to describe a combination of low growth, rising unemployment and inflation. Pulling the levers according to instruction no longer produced the desired result. Between 1968 and 1970 retail prices rose by average of 5.9 per cent per year, partly as a consequence of the inflationary effects of the Vietnam War. Between 1970 and 1973 the average annual increase was running at 8.6 per cent. During the same period there was a worrying increase in the numbers out of work. During the

Wilson Government of 1964−70 unemployment increased from 376,000 to 555,000. In 1972 it touched the psychologically important one million mark: 'Keynesian economics faced something of an intellectual crisis' (Kavanagh, 1987, p. 125).

The *relative* strength of the British economy was also giving cause for concern. The slow rate of British growth compared most unfavourably with that of some of the founder members of the EEC, particularly West Germany and France, though in reality this was part of a much longer-term problem going back to the last century (Marquand, 1988). By the early 1960s many were coming to realize that the notion of Britain as the world's third great power no longer had much meaning. Indeed, most converts to the idea of British membership of the European Community, on which issue a new consensus had been established by 1967, were moved by the straightforward desire to see Britain emulate her continental rivals, rather than by any deep-seated Europeanism.

It was the Conservative Party which made the first significant attacks on the postwar consensus. Of the Treasury ministers who resigned in 1958 it was Enoch Powell who emerged as the most articulate exponent of that libertarian, free-market Conservatism which had been largely submerged since the late 1940s. Particularly after his refusal to serve under Home in 1963 and again after his dismissal from Heath's Shadow Cabinet in 1968, Powell used his back-bench freedom to attack state intervention in the economy and to argue that government was the sole originator of inflation through its excessive spending. To begin with, his free-market, monetary policies were usually dismissed as an unrealistic throwback to the *laissez-faire* philosophy of the nineteenth century. Another sign was the foundation of the right-wing Monday Club in 1961. Its members were dismayed by Macmillan's famous 'Wind of Change' speech of February 1960, in which the Prime Minister had drawn attention to the imminent demise of European colonialism. Opposed to the liberal consensus on coloured immigration, they believed that under the influence of men such as Butler and Macmillan Conservatism had moved so far to the left that there was little to choose between the two major parties. Apart from attacking Labour's competence to govern, there seemed no scope for genuine party differentiation. Though they never fully coalesced, influences such as Powell and the Monday Club helped to move the party's position to the right after the election defeat of 1964. To continue with policies virtually indistinguishable from Labour's only made sense if the electorate continued to vote for the Conservative version of the consensus. Once in opposition the Conservatives had little room for manoeuvre except by moving to the right, if the electorate was ever going to be offered a real choice again. The change was apparent in the policy document *Putting Britain Right Ahead*, published in October 1965. With little mention of NEDC or incomes policies, it stressed ideas of competition and incentives.

Much of this new thinking was embraced in the Conservative manifesto for the 1966 General Election, *Action not Words*. There were proposals to reduce income tax, offer greater incentives to managers, break up monopolies, increase competition, join the EEC and move towards a more selective provision of welfare benefits. Much of this foreshadowed the Conservatism of Keith Joseph and Margaret Thatcher. But there was an important difference. Though the party had moved distinctly to the right, and while many now thought Butskellism was dead as far as the Conservative Party was concerned, the motive force was practical rather than ideological. Heath, who had taken a large personal part in the policy rethink, was himself firmly in the 'One Nation' tradition of postwar Conservatism. According to Keith Joseph, Heath's government of 1970 still adopted 'a statist approach, though with a huge emphasis on releasing entrepreneurship, on reforming trade unions and on sharpening competition' (Joseph, 1987, p. 28). The new policies reflected Heath's belief that Britain was sliding remorselessly downhill and that drastic action was necessary to reverse the trend. 'It was the product not of a right-wing ideology, but of an efficiency expert' (Lindsay and Harrington, 1979, p. 244). 'Are you moving at all to the right?' a friend is said to have asked Heath in 1970. 'Just a bit,' he replied, 'but we have to stay in the centre' (quoted in Whitehead, 1985, p. 40). Significantly, it was crucial to Heath's plans that government ministries, local government and the NHS should all be restructured in the interests of efficiency.

Seldom, if ever, in the twentieth century has a prospective government prepared its policies so thoroughly as Heath's Conservative Party did before the 1970 General Election. After the 1966 election there was considerable debate within the party on the question of an incomes policy, with the majority now siding with Enoch Powell in the belief that this was not a proper function of government. The failure of Labour's *In Place of Strife* in 1969 opened up a significant rift between the parties on how to deal with the power of the trade unions. It became for a time the deepest point of conflict between Labour and the Conservatives, with the latter determined to press on where Labour had drawn back and introduce a legal framework into industrial relations. With a growing sense of personal antipathy, particularly between their leaders, the two parties seemed to be moving away from their commitment to consensus.

Members of Heath's Shadow Cabinet met to put the finishing touches to their policies amid a glare of publicity at Selsdon Park in January 1970. Little emerged that had not been said before, apart perhaps from a renewed emphasis on tougher law and order measures. Wilson, however, seeing electoral advantage in emphasizing the extent of political polarization, was able to make great play with the idea of 'Selsdon Man' – the hard-hearted face of the new Conservatism, a reactionary opponent of social welfare and the planned economy. In February 1970 the Prime Minister declared, 'It is not just a lurch to the Right, it is an atavistic desire to reverse the course of 25 years of social revolution' (James, 1972, p. 214).

Against the predictions of most opinion polls, Heath became Prime Minister in June 1970 with a comfortable overall majority of thirty seats. The new government seemed determined to give the country policies that were fundamentally different from any seen since 1945. The new Conservatism was intended to be bracing and stimulating. For the individual there would be more take-home pay, but he would also have to do more for himself. Only those who could not would be protected by a

67

safety net of selective benefits. Whatever Heath's true intentions, the government seemed to be more right-wing than any since before the war, particularly after the sudden death of Iain Macleod, the Chancellor of the Exchequer, only a month after the General Election. It was in economic and industrial policy that the change was most marked. The new government hoped to reduce public expenditure and opposed wage and price regulation, together with state intervention in industry. The tone was set in a speech at the Party Conference in November 1970 by John Davies, catapulted as a consequence of Macleod's death to the new super-ministry of Trade and Industry. Davies clearly believed he was embarking on an industrial policy to break the postwar consensus of planning and intervention: 'I will not bolster up or bail out companies where I can see no end to the process of propping them up.' Government would no longer rush to the rescue of industrial lame ducks.

Reform of the trade unions was crucial to Heath's plans in order to sweep away ancient restrictive practices which were impeding the performance of British industry. Although the Industrial Relations Bill of 1971 was similar in many ways to that envisaged by Wilson and Castle in 1969, the Labour Party opposed it vehemently. The bill took up 450 hours of parliamentary time. In practice, however, the new act proved unworkable. It had been poorly drafted and had little hope of acceptance in the atmosphere of the early 1970s. The trade unions were largely able to ignore its provisions simply by refusing to register under the act, a development which the government seems not to have foreseen.

Despite the careful preparation of the years in opposition, most of Heath's policies went badly wrong. Membership of the EEC was secured — at a heavy price — in 1973, but as far as the economy was concerned all the vital indicators continued to move in the wrong direction. Industrial relations had never been worse in the whole postwar era and the government was humiliated by the miners' strike of 1972. Heath was particularly shaken when unemployment reached one million early in 1972. In general Heath's experience showed the extent to which the effective management of the national economy in the modern era lies outside the control of any government and at the mercy of international forces.

As early as 1971 a massive U-turn was under way. Rolls Royce, in difficulties over supplying engines for the Lockheed RB211 aircraft, was nationalized. Early in 1972 the same remedy was applied to the ailing Upper Clyde Shipbuilders. The budget of 1972 cut taxation and allowed public expenditure and government borrowing to rise. The Chancellor, Anthony Barber, announced the setting up of an Industrial Development Executive with powers to inject money into industrial investment. By August a powerfully interventionist Industry Bill was on the statute book, a complete reversal of the policy upon which the government had been elected. By the end of the year a formal incomes policy was in operation. It was as if a government which had had the temerity to deviate from the centre ground was now rushing back to the consensus politics of the early 1960s as fast as it could travel. Barber's dash for growth resembled the policy of the last Conservative Government, though its consequences proved even more inflationary.

Despite its change of course, success still eluded Heath's government. Buffeted by the Arab-Israeli War of 1973 and the subsequent quadrupling of oil prices, the government finally collapsed amidst the ignominy of the three-day week and another defeat at the hands of the miners. But the circumstances of Heath's fall would be of long-term importance for the consensus.

The years after 1970 also saw important developments inside the Labour Party. Not for the first time in its history, the party moved distinctly to the left during its period of opposition, abandoning many of the policies pursued by the last Wilson Government. The trend was particularly marked in the party outside Parliament, which seemed to be gaining greater influence in the party's decision-making processes. Tony Benn's chairmanship of the party in 1971–2 was the decisive period. Benn emerged as a populist champion of the left, speaking out for more public ownership and greater worker participation in industry. If Wilson's government had tried to practise the revisionist socialism of Anthony Crosland, it could scarcely claim to have done so successfully. By 1975 Stuart Holland's *The Challenge of Socialism* had produced a left-wing critique of Crosland's analysis.

Within a year of electoral defeat in 1970 the Labour Party as a whole had moved strongly against the EEC, although the leadership continued to stress that the terms of membership negotiated would be the critical factor. In reaction to the Heath Government's Industrial Relations Act, a liaison committee was set up in 1972 between the unions, the party's National Executive Committee and the parliamentary party. This produced the so-called Social Contract by which the unions promised to co-operate in controlling wages in return for government action on prices and a 'social wage' in terms of increased welfare benefits and other reforms. An enthusiast noted: 'The only way was to turn [trade union bargaining] power into something more positive by involving unions in the responsibilities of economic management' (Castle, 1980, p. 9). 'Labour's Programme for Britain, 1973' set forth the party's most radical agenda since the war, centred on a National Enterprise Board and a system of compulsory planning agreements with private industry. Under the next Labour government the frontiers of state ownership would make their first substantial advance since the late 1940s. Labour now promised a fundamental and irreversible shift in the distribution of wealth to working people and their families.

Not surprisingly, the movement away from the centre ground in first the Conservative Party (1965–72) and then Labour (1970–4) resulted in a marked period of adversarial politics. Opposition for opposition's sake seemed to be the order of the day and there was a bitterness in political debate which made it difficult to imagine that the consensus was still in being. Another inevitable consequence was a revival in the fortunes of the Liberal Party by the winter of 1972–3, with much talk of the need for a realignment of British politics to produce an effective 'Centre Party'.

At least for the purposes of this study it is possible to discern striking similarities between the Labour Government which

70

came into power (without an overall parliamentary majority) in 1974 and Heath's government of 1970. Both were determined, although in very different ways, to break away from the consensus politics of the postwar era. Labour entered office with a series of policies more radical than any endorsed by the party since 1945. According to David Coates, 'the shift to the left in language and programme after 1970 was on a scale last seen . . . as long ago as 1931' (Coates, 1980, p. 2). Though there was a remarkable continuity of personnel from the Labour Government which had lost power in June 1970 − in particular Wilson was once again Prime Minister − the presence of key left-wingers at the departments of Employment (Michael Foot) and Industry (Tony Benn) indicated a significant change of course. Yet the history of Wilson's government closely paralleled that of Heath's to the extent that the radical promise was largely frustrated. According to one left-wing critic, 'with the election [of October 1974] over, and in the face of persistent inflation, low rates of investment, heavy foreign debts and periodic currency crises, the Labour government slipped imperceptibly but steadily away from what the left of the Party had held to be the radical promise of the opposition years' (Coates, 1980, p. 11).

Labour won the two general elections of 1974 primarily on its claim that it could work successfully with the trade unions. The bitter confrontations of the period 1971−4 had re-established Labour's claim to enjoy a special relationship with the trade unions, notwithstanding the brief interlude surrounding *In Place of Strife* in 1969. Moreover, it had been the left-wing trade union leaders who had, via the bloc vote, provided crucial support for the adoption of Labour's new programme at the vital party conferences of the early 1970s. The repeal of the Tories' hated Industrial Relations Act was central to Labour's programme. It would not be necessary. The Social Contract would allow for a superior and more fruitful relationship with the unions. Certainly Labour proceeded to identify itself more closely with the trade union movement than had its predecessors in 1945 and 1964. Wilson's first meeting after becoming Prime Minister was with the General Council of the TUC. Foot

71

quickly settled the miners' strike: at 29 per cent the settlement involved few concessions from the National Union of Miners. He remained throughout a reliable champion of the workers' cause in government. Some argued, with a little exaggeration, that Congress House became virtually a department of government. One opinion poll revealed the public's perception that Jack Jones had become the most powerful man in the land.

Opinions on the Social Contract are, however, varied. One Treasury minister was scathing: 'To my mind the only give and take in the contract was that the government gave and the unions took' (J. Barnett, 1982, p. 49). By contrast a socialist critic argued that, within a year, crude wage restraint became the centrepiece of the contract, while the government's part in terms of radical policies in the fields of industrial relations, industrial democracy, investment, housing, prices and social benefits was largely abandoned (Coates, 1980, p. 82). What seems less open to dispute is that the contract singularly failed to provide a satisfactory basis for the management of the economy. Within its first year inflation soared to 27 per cent. By June 1975 earnings had increased by an average of 26.6 per cent and weekly wage rates by 33 per cent. There was serious concern that the economy was out of control and in July 1975 a formal incomes policy was introduced. By October 1975 the British economy was producing less than at any time since 1970, while unemployment had passed the seasonally adjusted one million mark. Over the previous three years public expenditure had grown by almost a fifth, while output had risen by less than 2 per cent. Public spending now accounted for a massive 60 per cent of Gross Domestic Product.

Also central to Labour's strategy as worked out in Opposition was the role of the National Enterprise Board. Its functions were to help establish and develop particular industries, extend public ownership into profitable manufacturing industries, and promote industrial democracy. The government's Industry Bill was passed in November 1975 and by early 1976 companies which had come wholly or partly into public ownership included Ferranti, Alfred Herbert, British Leyland and Triang. Overall, however, the emphasis of the government's industrial policy moved away from intervention and control and towards the conventional ideas of exhortation and support. The NEB became less the vehicle for a major shift in the ownership of British industry than a rescue agent for ailing firms.

Broadly speaking, the failure of Labour's leftward lurch may be explained by two factors, one domestic and one external. Despite the presence of men such as Foot and Benn − and Benn was moved to the less sensitive Energy department in June 1975 − the majority of the Cabinet were of the party's right and centre, making the translation of Labour's 1973 programme into reality always somewhat problematical. Labour's constitutional structure generally allows the parliamentary party to reassert its authority over extra-parliamentary groupings once Labour is in government. The crucial appointment was that of Denis Healey as Chancellor. His budget speech of November 1974 revealed him to be an orthodox chancellor pursuing orthodox budgetary targets. Chancellor throughout the Labour Government, from 1974 to 1979, Healey received the sort of abuse from Labour's left wing that is usually reserved for the most hated Tory. But the external factor was perhaps even more important. As with Heath's government before it, Labour's policy options were severely circumscribed by the state of the world economy. In the face of the massive oil price increases of 1973 Healey at first decided to maintain Labour's public spending plans and to borrow to meet the deficit (J. Barnett, 1982, p. 23). Soon, however, the balance-of-payments deficit came to constrain the government at every turn. To deal with it became a prime object of the government's policy. But massive borrowing meant that foreign creditors held the whip hand over the British economy because of their ability to withdraw their loans or move out of sterling on a huge scale. As the world moved into recession, one nation after another gave up the struggle to sustain growth and reverted to deflationary policies. Short of retreating behind an Eastern European style siege economy, the British government had little alternative but to follow suit.

But the world had ceased responding to a recession with the traditional Keynesian methods. The new policies of monetarism were in vogue. The control of inflation had overtaken the maintenance of full employment in the hierarchy of economic objectives. By 1975 Labour was in danger of leaving the post-war consensus behind, but not in the sense intended when the government had taken office only a year before. In his budget of March 1975 Denis Healey effectively abandoned the commitment to full employment. Instead of spending his way out of recession, Healey proposed to reduce the government's deficit. It was an historic moment.

Labour's policies also underwent an about-turn on the central foreign policy issue of continued membership of the EEC. The party's special conference in April 1975 voted by a majority of two to one for withdrawal, but when a referendum was held in June the government recommended a 'yes' vote to the proposition of staying in, and the country accepted its advice. Thus, by the time of his sudden resignation in April 1976, Wilson had succeeded in turning his party 'towards Europe, incomes policy and the mixed economy' and away from the fundamentalist socialism of the 1973 programme (Whitehead, 1985, p. 154).

The new Labour Prime Minister, James Callaghan, experienced a baptism of fire. The year 1976 saw the explicit and almost total abandonment of the goals with which Labour had begun its term of office. Healey's spring budget indicated that he had accepted a monetarist solution to the country's problems. In July a package of spending cuts was announced, accompanied by a rise in interest rates and a statement from the Chancellor that monetary growth should be restricted to 12 per cent in 1976–7. Such measures, however, were not sufficient to prevent a dramatic fall in the value of the pound, leading the government to seek a loan of nearly four billion dollars from the International Monetary Fund. To achieve this subvention the government was forced to accept further increases in taxation and cuts in public expenditure. Philip Whitehead comments: 'It looked to Labour activists then, and seems in memory now, like the death of Keynesian welfare socialism and the birth of monetarism, the external dictatorship of the markets and the American bankers' (Whitehead, 1985, p. 200).

A speech which Callaghan delivered at the Lord Mayor's banquet in November indicated how far Labour had travelled since 1973:

> We must make a success of the mixed economy by adhering to an industrial strategy worked out and agreed by both the T.U.C. and the C.B.I., which aimed at giving absolute priority to industrial needs ahead of even our social objectives. (quoted in Coates, 1980, p. 35)

But his speech to the Party Conference in September, disavowing any faith in Keynesian demand management, showed how far Labour had come in the years since 1945:

> We used to think that you could just spend your way out of recession and increase employment only by cutting taxes and boosting government expenditure ... it only worked by injecting bigger doses of inflation into the economy followed by a higher level of unemployment at the next step ... the option [of spending yourself out of a recession] no longer exists. (quoted in Kavanagh and Morris, 1989, p. 42)

Throughout its life the Wilson-Callaghan Government enjoyed only a precarious parliamentary existence. From 1977−8 its continuation in office depended on a pact with the Liberal Party of David Steel. Despite some temporary success in controlling wage rises, the government ultimately fell, rather as Heath's had done, the victim of its own incomes strategy after the celebrated 'winter of discontent'. As Margaret Thatcher took office as Britain's first woman Prime Minister in May 1979, thirty-four years had elapsed since the end of the Second World War. Those years had been divided equally between Labour and Conservative governments. However history comes finally to judge this period, there were few in 1979, on left or

75

right, who believed that either party had yet found the appropriate policies to deal with Britain's problems. If a consensus still existed in 1979, it was perhaps that the time was ripe for a genuinely new beginning.

5

The Consensus Overthrown, 1979–87

Mrs Thatcher made something of a virtue of her determination to break the postwar consensus. To an audience in Cardiff in April 1979 she announced:

> I am a conviction politician. The Old Testament prophets did not say 'Brothers, I want a consensus'. They said 'This is my faith. This is what I passionately believe. If you believe it too, then come with me.' (quoted in Rose, 1980, p. 4)

Two years later she dismissed the idea of consensus as 'the process of abandoning all beliefs, principles, values and policies ... avoiding the very issues that have got to be solved merely to get people to come to an agreement on the way ahead' (quoted in Kavanagh and Morris, 1989, p. 119). The destruction of the consensus would, she hoped, one day become one of the lasting achievements for which she would be remembered. The reason for her hostility was clear. In her mind consensus was equated with the appeasement of socialism and the progressive advance of collectivism since 1945. By it, Tories had connived in inflation and allowed the government to be dictated to by the trade unions. That process had now not simply to be stopped, but actually reversed. Not surprisingly, two obviously 'socialist' elements in the consensus — the nationalized industries and trade union power — would be special objects of her government's assault.

If the consensus had enjoyed greater success during the years of its ascendancy, it would have been less vulnerable to frontal attack in 1979. But 'there is no gainsaying that the first thirty postwar years of consensus politics coincided with both a steady reduction in Britain's international standing and a relative economic decline' (Kavanagh, 1987, p. 57). The country had achieved a lower rate of economic growth than most other industrial nations. It was a trend which one government after another had pledged itself to reverse, but without success. 'Many of the ideas and policies identified with the post-war consensus gradually came to be regarded as causes and symptoms of Britain's decline' (Kavanagh, 1987, p. 124). In absolute terms, the audit of Britain's economic performance was much less bleak. In every year from 1945 to 1973, with the exception of 1958, the British economy had grown. The result had been the most rapid rise in living standards and social welfare provision in the country's history. The most recent experience, however, had been less satisfactory. During the 1970s British unemployment had trebled, while inflation rose twice as fast as it did in the average of the OECD (Organization for Economic Co-operation and Development) countries. Not surprisingly, there was by the end of the decade a profound feeling of pessimism about Britain's future. Richard Rose, in a book symbolically entitled *Do Parties Make a Difference?*, suggested that, whoever was in office in the 1980s, 'the problems of the British economy may become even worse than before' (Rose, 1980, p. 140).

Both the Conservative Government of 1970 and its Labour successor of 1974 had, of course, been just as pledged as Mrs Thatcher to break the mould of postwar politics. Each had failed. James Callaghan warned that Mrs Thatcher's arrival presaged far more than the 'normal change of policies' associated with the election of a new government. With the inevitable exaggeration of political rhetoric, he continued: 'What we are seeing today is an attempt to take us back to the nineteenth century' (quoted in Rose, 1980, p. 157). Others, however, drawing on past experience, were sceptical about the new government's ability to effect a long-term change in the direction of British politics. In April 1979 the editor of the *Sunday Telegraph* predicted that 'Whatever happens in the election is not going to make much difference. There will be neither revolution nor counter-revolution.' Any change would be measured 'in inches not miles' (quoted in Kavanagh, 1987, p. 207). If Mrs Thatcher were to succeed, momentarily, in striking out in new directions, it was widely assumed that she too, like Heath in 1972 and Callaghan in 1976, would be brought back towards the centre via an inevitable U-turn. But the Thatcher Revolution was more closely in tune with the social, economic and intellectual mood of its time than had been the experiments of her predecessors. It is therefore necessary to say something of the emergence of the New Right in Conservative thinking.

The 1979 Conservative manifesto bore some striking similarities to that of 1970. Both, for example, stressed the invigorating power of the market economy. But Mrs Thatcher's Conservatism was much more firmly based both in economic theory and ideological vision than had been Heath's flirtation with the political right between 1965 and 1972. By about 1973 inflation had taken over from unemployment as the most pressing problem of both the British and international economies. The perceived failure of Keynesianism by the mid-1970s cleared the way for the revival of an alternative economic theory that had lain largely dormant through the consensus years. The quest for a solution to inflation gave scope for the monetarist school of economists to enjoy a new vogue of popularity. Its most celebrated exponent was the American, Milton Friedman, awarded the Nobel Prize for Economics in 1976.

According to Friedman and the so-called 'Chicago School', inflation can only be cured by controlling the supply of money. In other words, money, like everything else, is subject to the laws of supply and demand. If, therefore, government creates an excessive supply of money, its value will fall and inflation result. In Britain an important role was played by the leading economic correspondents of the *Financial Times* and *The Times* in popularizing monetarist ideas. Both Samuel Brittan and Peter Jay were disillusioned Keynesians, only too conscious that existing policies no longer offered a choice between stable prices and unemployment. Also important in the intellectual origins of the New Right was the Austrian, Friedrich von Hayek. A distinguished economist himself – he was awarded the Nobel Prize in 1974 – it was Hayek's social philosophy, based on the centrality of the market and the threats to liberty posed by excessive government interference, which exercised most influence. Ironically his seminal work, *Road to Serfdom*, had been published as long ago as 1944, just as the consensus of Keynes and Beveridge came to fruition. Its central argument was that freedom and planning could not be combined.

The change of mood and attitude was an international phenomenon. Harold Wilson recalled a speech in 1976 by the German Social Democratic Chancellor, Helmut Schmidt: 'The Keynesian heresy had to be extirpated, and Milton Friedman at his best could not have excelled him' (Wilson, 1979, p. 237). Mrs. Thatcher's rise in Britain coincided with that of Ronald Reagan in the United States. In Britain the impact of the change was particularly marked both because the economic problems seemed more acute than elsewhere, and because of the intense disappointment which Conservatives experienced at the fate of the Heath Government – its U-turn in 1972 and the ignominy of its collapse two years later. Enoch Powell had spoken of the inflationary effects of Heath's policies. In June 1973 he warned that the money supply would increase by a fifth in a single year, with inevitable inflationary consequences. But Powell lacked a sufficient following inside the party to make much of an impression, and even refused to stand for re-election as a Conservative in February 1974. Another prophet was needed. Between the two elections of 1974 Sir Keith Joseph, Social Services Secretary in the recent government and still a member of Heath's Shadow Cabinet, began to develop a radical, agonized and increasingly public critique of Heath's style of Conservatism.

A patently sincere man, for a politician sometimes embarrassingly so, Joseph developed his analysis into a wide-ranging challenge to the whole direction of Britain's economic management since the war. He was not concerned to make party

80

political points, admitting that the new Labour Government's problems with inflation were largely the consequence of Barber's profligacy in the previous administration. In a vain attempt to sustain the consensus, past Conservative governments had made progressive concessions to socialism, so that the supposed centre ground of politics had moved ever further to the left. Tories had thus allowed the rules of the political game to be set by their opponents. This was the so-called ratchet effect. Joseph now called for a return to a free-market economy, the control of inflation by a strict monetary policy and extensive cuts in public expenditure. Perhaps his most important speech came at Preston during the election campaign of October 1974. Here he placed monetarism firmly on the political agenda as he singled out inflation, rather than unemployment, as the most important issue facing the country. Peter Jenkins comments: 'Here was Joseph seemingly abandoning the very goal [of full employment], tearing up the sacred Beveridge text' (Jenkins, 1987, p. 62).

Joseph's chances of succeeding Heath as Conservative leader were effectively destroyed by a further speech in Birmingham in which he seemed to some to imply that mothers from lower-class backgrounds should be encouraged to have fewer children, so that they would pose less of a burden for the welfare services. It was in these circumstances that Margaret Thatcher emerged to challenge Heath for the leadership in February 1975. As Education Secretary throughout Heath's government, she had been one of the Cabinet's high-spending ministers. But she had emerged as a willing recipient of Joseph's monetarist ideas and also, since the Tories lost office, as a formidable parliamentary performer in her capacity as a shadow Treasury spokesman. Her victory over Heath was only in part the expression of a swing to the right in the Conservative ranks. More important was a back-bench revolt against Heath as a political loser — he had lost three out of four general elections — and a man who had lost touch with his own MPs.

During the period 1975—9 the details of what became known as 'Thatcherism' were worked out. This involved the abandonment of the postwar consensus in many of its aspects and the creation of a very different socio-economic vision. This was all done very consciously. As Nigel Lawson later put it: 'Our chosen course does represent a distinct and self-conscious break from the predominantly social democratic assumptions that have hitherto underlain policy in post-war Britain' (quoted in Kavanagh, 1987, p. 13). It was much more than just picking up the ideas which Heath had abandoned in 1972. The consensus had produced a regime of high taxation, over-mighty trade unions and overmanned and inefficient industries. At the same time the Welfare State had degenerated into a dependency culture in which people relied too heavily on the state provision of benefits, thereby destroying initiative and enterprise. In this way economic decline and social decadence were linked as associated evils. The New Right looked to the way in which countries such as West Germany and Japan, which made a point of emphasizing free enterprise, had done much better than Britain in the same period. Thatcherism looked therefore to the market rather than the state to allocate resources. It vehemently opposed the sort of state activities which the Butskellite consensus had taken for granted. The individual must show a sense of responsibility and a spirit of enterprise for Britain to become competitive again in relation to other countries. That enterprise would be rewarded by tax cuts to allow those who risked their capital to keep a larger share of resulting profits. This rethink went on in a favourable intellectual environment. Bodies such as the Adam Smith Institute, the Centre for Policy Studies and the Institute for Economic Affairs acted as think-tanks for the idea that only capitalism could guarantee the freedom of the individual and that the long march of collectivism had to be reversed.

Within the Conservative Party, however, Mrs Thatcher and Sir Keith had to tread warily. Most of their senior colleagues were sceptical of, and in some cases hostile to, the new ideas. The policy document, 'The Right Approach to the Economy', published in 1977, was something of a compromise, but it was noticeable that the party's 1979 manifesto, for the first time since the war, avoided any commitment to full employment. This was despite its effective use of the slogan 'Labour isn't working' as a commentary on existing levels of unemployment. The Conservative victory in 1979 is most properly viewed as a massive vote of no confidence in the outgoing Labour Government, rather than a popular endorsement of the ideas of the New Right. As has been seen, many did not believe that Mrs Thatcher would in practice be able to give a significantly different turn to the direction of British politics. Cabinet sceptics were confident of their ability to keep the government in the traditional centre ground. James Prior, Employment Secretary in the new government, later recalled: 'I thought that we would at least be able to avoid most of the follies which new Governments tend to commit and that we wouldn't be stupidly right-wing and doctrinaire about economic policy, as we had been between 1970 and 1972' (Prior, 1986, p. 115). But the key posts in the economic ministries were held by true believers who had fully recanted the politics and policies of the consensus. Most important were Joseph at Industry and Sir Geoffrey Howe, the new Chancellor.

The historian steps at his peril into the events of the most recent decade. The quests for objectivity and perspective are intrinsic to his craft and assessments of the very recent past must be recognized as hesitant and provisional. Certainly it is too soon to attempt a definitive judgement on the achievements of the Thatcher years and the extent to which she has succeeded in changing the course of postwar British history. Opinions at the moment are divided. Dennis Kavanagh concludes that the Conservatives' record since 1979 is one which has fallen short of the hopes of their more radical supporters, but that substantial changes have occurred 'compared with other governments since 1951' (Kavanagh, 1987, p. 244). According to Peter Riddell, the first Thatcher Government (1979–83) fell short of most of its central objectives (Riddell, 1983), but Martin Holmes credits it with changing the parameters of political and economic debate so markedly as to render impossible a return to the days of Keynesian consensus (Holmes, 1985b).

It is certainly true that, as with most governments, Mrs Thatcher's has been stronger on rhetoric than achievement. Policy on public expenditure is the most interesting example of this. The government's goals were subtly modified as the years went by. The original policy of 1979 was to reduce expenditure in real terms. The Medium Term Financial Strategy was all important. But the welfare costs of mounting unemployment and an increasingly ageing population left little scope for real overall savings. By 1984 policy was merely to contain spending in real terms. By 1986 it was to ensure that growing public expenditure should decline as a percentage of a faster growing Gross Domestic Product. This was something which the Labour Government had actually achieved in 1975–6 and 1977–8. Policy on the control of inflation has undergone similar revision. There was no spectacular U-turn, as many thought would be inevitable. Despite mounting unemployment which topped three million by January 1982, Howe's 1981 budget was a watershed. In the middle of a massive recession he eschewed Keynesian remedies and opted for further deflation. Controlling inflation remained pre-eminent among the government's priorities and probably still does. But the government seemed to abandon straightforward Friedmanite monetarism after about 1983, when Nigel Lawson succeeded Howe as Chancellor, largely because of the difficulty of finding an accurate and reliable measure of the money supply. Present (1990) anti-inflationary policy focuses primarily on the use of interest rates.

Yet it would be misleading to underplay the changes which have occurred since 1979 and the extent to which these changes have destroyed the fundamental assumptions of postwar politics. David Butler is surely right to argue that the General Election of 1979 produced the most decisive changes of any election since the war (D. Butler, 1989, p. 114). The New Right was aware that many of its ideas were in no sense original, and this book has attempted to record some of the challenges to the consensus which preceded Mrs Thatcher's arrival on the scene. She recognized this herself. Her appointment as party chairman in 1975 of the almost forgotten Peter Thorneycroft, the Chancellor who had resigned in 1958 on the issue of sound money, was eloquent recognition of the continuities in the Thatcher Revolution. But Mrs Thatcher saw her task as to carry on where others had only pointed the way.

There is, of course, a case for pointing to 1976 rather than 1979 as the real break with the postwar consensus (Holmes, 1985a, p. 163). Counter-inflation policy was first given priority over employment under Callaghan. Monetary targets had first been set by Denis Healey. Callaghan's disavowal of Keynesian economics in his conference speech of 1976 has already been noted. Massive spending cuts were imposed by Labour, and in many respects the Conservatives' spending priorities after 1979 were not significantly different from those planned by Callaghan's outgoing government (Kavanagh, 1987, p. 229). One Marxist critic has argued that the growth of the Welfare State came to an end in 1976 rather than 1979 (Gough, 1979, ch. 7). But there is an important difference: 'There is no evidence that Labour ministers . . . were convinced by monetarist arguments' (Peden, 1985, p. 221). More probably they were deliberately talking the language which those from whom they wished to borrow wanted to hear. In so far as Labour had abandoned Keynesian expansionism, this was regarded as only a temporary expedient until the economic climate improved. For Mrs Thatcher, on the other hand, there would be no going back. Certainly the Labour Cabinet of 1976 which accepted the IMF's terms did not share the socio-political vision which for Conservatives such as Joseph and Mrs Thatcher was an intrinsic part of the new approach.

The 'Thatcher Revolution' has had an uneven impact. Policy towards the nationalized industries is an area which has seen a particularly marked break with the postwar consensus. During the Attlee Government something like 20 per cent of the economy was taken into state control. As has been seen, Conservative governments from Churchill to Douglas-Home kept the vast majority of nationalized industries in the public sector. The mixed economy seemed to be a permanent feature of the postwar landscape. Even the Heath Government had little success in turning back the clock. Thomas Cook and Son was sold off, while the Coal Board was told to denationalize its brickworks and British Rail its hotels. But such tinkering around the edges has to be set against the massive rescue operations launched for Rolls Royce and Upper Clyde Shipbuilders. Nor

85

in fact was the concept of privatization widely discussed in the period of policy planning under Mrs Thatcher, 1975—9 (Morgan, 1988, p. 34). The first Thatcher Government saw some measures of denationalization, but only after the successful sale of British Telecom in 1984 was there a significant increase of momentum. This was followed by a wave of privatizations, culminating in the sale of the gas industry in December 1986 and BP a year later. Water has recently crossed over into the private sector, electricity is soon to follow and there are now promises that a future Tory government will sell off the coal mines and possibly the railways. Little of this would have been thought possible as recently as 1979. One enthusiast has written of 'the largest transfer of property since the dissolution of the monasteries under Henry VIII, a transfer from the state to its citizens' (M. Pirie, quoted in Kavanagh, 1987, p. 221). In the process the government has succeeded in creating a large number of new private share-owners and in financing tax cuts and debt repayment, though the difficulty of introducing the bracing winds of competition into what are mostly natural monopolies has been a limiting factor in any comparison between the rhetoric and the achievement of the privatization programme.

Policy towards the trade unions is another area where the discontinuities after 1979 are particularly marked. As has been seen, throughout the postwar era Conservative governments as much as Labour took the trade union movement very seriously. Even Edward Heath, despite the confrontational aspects of the Industrial Relations Act, strove mightily to establish a good relationship with union leaders and to secure TUC co-operation for his incomes policy from 1972 onwards. The New Right held the trade unions as partly responsible for Britain's relatively poor industrial performance since the war. Influenced particularly by Heath's experience with the miners in 1972 and again in 1974, Mrs Thatcher did not believe that the unions had any particular claim to recognition in the corridors of power. They were 'simply the unacceptable face of corporatism, the epitome of all that was bad about the hated post-war settlement' (Taylor, 1989, p. 23). After 1979 the TUC came to exercise an increasingly negligible influence over government policy. The era of convivial co-operation between government and unions — 'beer and sandwiches at No. 10' had been the characteristic of the Wilson years — was at an end. Most importantly, of course, the unions were confronted by a government which did not look upon the maintenance of full employment as an overriding priority.

Not only was it necessary to exclude the unions from the government's policy-making processes. The balance of power in industrial relations had to be radically changed in favour of management if British industry was to become more efficient and competitive. The Conservatives proceeded more cautiously than had Heath in 1971 and with better considered legislation. The cautious approach was particularly evident while James Prior was Employment Secretary, 1979—81. But over a period of time acts were put on to the statute book which severely limited union power in relation to secondary strike action and picketing, while introducing a more democratic and open structure into the unions' own affairs. At the time of writing, further legislation is promised to outlaw the closed shop and to restrict unofficial strikes. In a period of very high unemployment the unions proved incapable of mounting any effective opposition against the government's proposals and even the year-long miners' strike of 1984—5 was successfully defeated.

If the nationalized industries and the trade union movement offer examples of radical change effected by the Thatcher Government, policies towards the Welfare State and education still show the persistent strength of the consensus. The New Right's case was clear enough. Britain had become trapped in a vicious circle with the Welfare State swallowing up an ever higher proportion of national wealth and encouraging the citizen to look too readily to the state rather than his own initiative to provide for his needs. Increasing costs resulted in higher taxes and accelerating wage inflation. Though the Thatcher Government has spoken of the need for the individual to stop turning to government for a solution to all his problems, and while there has been some movement towards a more selective provision of welfare benefits, the fundamental structure of the Beveridge system remains largely intact, particularly the National

Health Service. To date the political costs of a more radical approach have been deemed too high. The electorate has proved far more wedded to this aspect of the postwar consensus than to many others, and for some years the government has been anxious to reiterate that the NHS is 'safe in its hands'. Broadly speaking, the same picture emerges in the field of education. The comprehensive restructuring of the 1960s and 1970s remains essentially intact and the government has drawn back from the idea of a consumer-orientated system based on educational vouchers. Health, social security and education are still seen as proper areas of state responsibility.

Just as the creation of the postwar consensus required *both* parties to move towards a common centre ground, so too its destruction is best understood in terms of *both* parties retreating from this point of convergence. The emergence of a New Right within the Tory Party was matched by the renaissance of the left in Labour's ranks. By 1979 both were ready to condemn the consensus and see within it the seeds of Britain's decline. Both would have agreed that whichever party had been nominally in office since 1945, in practice social democracy had been in power. Thereafter, of course, their analyses diverged. While the right believed that Britain had been brought to her knees by a stultifying collectivism, the left discerned a crisis, possibly terminal, of the whole capitalist system. As the right's analysis was strengthened by the experience of the Heath Government, the left drew equally compelling evidence from the Wilson-Callaghan years. Socialism and the class struggle had been betrayed while Labour governments sought to prop up the failing edifice of capitalism. Suddenly Aneurin Bevan's criticisms of the consensus, voiced back in 1944, assumed a new relevance. The Crosland vision of how to achieve a socialist society had now to be jettisoned. As in the early 1970s, Tony Benn was the most important figure in Labour's swing to the left. According to Peter Jenkins, 'Thatcher and Benn formed unholy alliance to dance on the grave of John Maynard Keynes' (Jenkins, 1987, p. 51).

So traumatic was the experience of the last months of

Callaghan's government, with Labour locked in conflict with its supposed comrades in the trade union movement, that it was not difficult to move the party rapidly to the left, with the annual conference and the National Executive Committee (NEC) achieving unprecedented power over the direction of policy. The time was now ripe for a truly socialist strategy. The election of the veteran left-winger, Michael Foot, to succeed Callaghan as party leader in 1980 was a sign of the times. Yet even Foot was embarrassed by the selection of parliamentary candidates such as Pat Wall and Peter Tatchell and the evident advance of the so-called Militant Tendency within the party's ranks.

For some time the left had been making steady progress within the Labour movement at the grass-roots constituency level. Here a type of militant party activist had risen to prominence, whose politics had little in common with those of the average Labour voter − or even with the Labour Party of Attlee, Gaitskell and Wilson. The party leadership had chosen largely to ignore what many saw as a scarcely concealed form of entryism into Labour's ranks by people whose adherence to the traditions of democratic socialism was open to grave question. But the experience of Labour politics in cities such as Liverpool stood as an indication of the direction in which the party might now head. It was in such circumstances that leading right-wingers such as Roy Jenkins and David Owen left to form the Social Democratic Party (SDP) in 1981.

On the basis of his support among constituency activists Tony Benn reached new heights of influence within Labour's ranks, culminating in his narrow defeat by Denis Healey in the election for the party's deputy leadership in September 1981. With little difficulty Labour abandoned many of the policies which had been pursued by its own government. In contrast to the New Right, Labour's departure from the consensus affected its attitude to foreign and defence policy, as well as economic matters. By 1981, in addition to massive increases in public expenditure and public ownership, and the effective adoption of the left's 'Alternative Economic Strategy', which the Labour Cabinet had successfully resisted when in government, the

Party Conference endorsed unilateral nuclear disarmament, withdrawal from the EEC and the closure of American nuclear bases in Britain. Even the national constitution, an unspoken assumption of the consensus, seemed under threat as Labour pledged itself to abolish the House of Lords. Not surprisingly, David Butler concludes that the 1983 election 'offered the widest choice of any postwar contest' (D. Butler, 1989, p. 114). Though Labour softened the presentation of its policies in 1987 and, in the person of Neil Kinnock, presented them under a more electable leader, the gap between the two main parties remained wide. The consensus was in fact dead.

6

Towards a New Consensus, 1987—?

The central argument of this book has been that the political consensus was largely a product of the experience of the Second World War (though its shape was by no means complete in 1945), and that it dominated the 1950s and 1960s, surviving into the 1970s under increasing strain. But the term had ceased to be a useful framework of historical analysis by the time of the general election of 1979. The consensus collapsed in the face of the emergence of new problems to which it appeared not to have the answers, and in the light of increasing evidence that it could not even tackle those problems which it had once seemed purpose-built to resolve.

The story is incomplete to the extent that the Labour Party has not regained power to be able to implement its alternative to the consensus politics of earlier years. Indeed, it is possible that had a Labour Government been elected in 1983 or 1987 it would have been obliged, like its predecessor of 1974, to trim its socialist sails in the face of the realities of the prevailing situation. It has, after all, been one of the purposes of this book to stress the differences which often occur between what a party says in Opposition and what in practice it does in power. The result might well have been a centrist government in the Wilson-Callaghan mould, which could even have been forced to embrace some of the ideas of the New Right after the fashion of the Labour governments in Australia and New Zealand in the same period.

Be that as it may, there have been signs over the last few years of the possible emergence of a new consensus. Like that which had developed by 1951, it involves a movement by both parties towards a common ground. The earlier consensus was firmly fixed in a centre-left position; its successor is of the centre-right. In both cases an important factor in its creation is the adaptation of one party to electoral defeat. Labour's three successive losses — in 1979 and more particularly in 1983 and 1987 — have had a sobering effect. Any party which aspires to government must take account of the lessons of defeat and reflect upon the verdict of the voters. This is not surprising. As Quintin Hogg once wrote: 'There is no copyright in truth and what is controversial politics at one moment may after experience and reflection easily become common ground' (Hailsham, 1959, p. 16).

All but the implacable 'Hard Left' now seem convinced that Labour would never win with some of the policies presented to the electorate in 1983 and 1987. Ten years of government under Mrs Thatcher have had a remarkable effect in shifting the political goal-posts firmly, and possibly irreversibly, to the right, particularly since many governments across the world have behaved in a very similar fashion. Back in the 1970s Sir Keith Joseph spoke of the need to establish a new 'common ground' to the right of centre. There are signs that this is becoming a reality. There is evidence of a new set of parameters within which a future Labour government would have to operate. Most commentators agreed that Labour fought an effective campaign in the General Election of 1987. Its reward — barely 30 per cent of the popular vote — showed that it was Labour's policies which were the problem. The subsequent policy review has resulted in a Labour Party almost unrecognizable from the one which Michael Foot took into battle in 1983. Even before the review took place it was difficult to see a future Labour government being able completely to reverse the changes effected since 1979. Further nationalization had ceased to be practical politics. Labour could not reintroduce exchange controls in a world which has largely abandoned them. Any hopes of socialism in one country thus seem no more than a pipedream. The reduction in trade union power has proved so popular — even among trade unionists — that a Labour government would seek to turn back the clock at its peril. The once reviled policy of selling council houses also enjoys widespread support. No Labour government would pursue policies which ran the risk of inflation on the scale of the 1970s.

Some changes of attitude occurred fairly early on in the Thatcher era. When in 1981 the SDP called for a reinstatement of Keynesianism, Ralf Dahrendorf joked that the party seemed to be 'promising a better past'. That same year the TUC put forward a five-year programme for *The Reconstruction of Industry*. It was a reflection of its declining faith in Keynesian policies of public investment that the TUC's plan would have generated no more than half a million jobs in five years (Peden, 1985, p. 232).

Since 1987 the processes of policy reassessment have gone on apace. Labour MPs have been keen to determine where they have offended electoral opinion. The policy review has produced dramatic changes. Labour's defence policy now stresses a multilateral approach to nuclear disarmament. The party seems to be wedded to the EEC and even enthusiastic about its Social Charter. Though each of the government's trade union laws has been bitterly opposed, it is now clear that most will not be repealed if Labour takes office. At the time of writing the party seems even to have reconciled itself to the abolition of the closed shop. A future Labour government will only place public utilities and natural monopolies under 'some form of social ownership', social ownership being Labour's attempt to reconcile the public interest with the natural working of the free market. Only the renationalization of British Telecom and water has been specifically pledged. Labour's deputy leader, Roy Hattersley, has argued the case for share ownership by trade union employees. Perhaps most surprisingly of all, Labour is now committed to a top rate of income tax of only 50 per cent — not very different from the Tories' 40 per cent, which it once condemned as retrogressive and immoral (Jones, 1989, p. 6; Kellner, 1989, p. 14).

One consequence of Labour's coming to terms with the new

realities has been the loss of support for the Social and Liberal Democrats since the 1987 election. When Labour and the Conservatives contest 'the middle ground', wherever that middle ground is placed on the political spectrum at any given moment, the centre parties have always been the most obvious casualties.

So future historians may well write of the rise and fall and rebirth of consensus politics, with 1979 as the pivotal year, just as 1945 was for an earlier era. That consensus will not imply, any more than did its predecessor, a total uniformity of outlook, policy and ambition between the two major parties. But Churchill's words to the American Congress in 1952 probably still hold true. While Labour's socialism and the Tories' free enterprise give plenty of room for argument, they 'fortunately overlap quite a lot in practice' (quoted in Ramsden, 1987, p. 52).

One final question clearly confronts the student of British politics since 1945. The debate over the very existence of a consensus is clearly one of considerable historical importance. In recent years, however, it has also taken on a contemporary political significance. Just as there is not full agreement on whether the consensus actually existed, there is no agreement among those who believe that it did exist on the effect which it had on Britain's postwar development. In short, was the consensus a good thing or not? The evidence is contradictory. On the one hand there can be no doubt that the period witnessed very substantial progress, not least in the material welfare of the British people. The creation of the Welfare State, so soon after the enormous sacrifices entailed in the Second World War, was itself no small achievement. Average real earnings rose by 20 per cent between 1951 and 1959, so that by the end of the decade Prime Minister Macmillan could, with some degree of justification, proclaim that 'most of our people have never had it so good'. Nor was this advance at the expense of the less fortunate in society. Between 1945 and 1970 unemployment, the great scourge of the inter-war era, averaged less than 3 per cent. Yet, in comparison with many of her competitors, this was also a period in which Britain's long-term relative decline accelerated. Between 1953 and 1960 the country's share of world manufactured exports fell from 20 to 15 per cent. Over the same period West Germany's share rose from 15 to 19 per cent. French exports increased three times as fast and West Germany's and Italy's six times as fast as did Britain's in these years. In 1945 Britain was rightly regarded as one of the world's great powers. By 1970 no serious observer could still maintain such a belief.

The argument goes yet further. It is possible to suggest that it was the policies of the consensus years which actually contributed to Britain's decline − that the policy-makers of the 1950s and 1960s failed to grapple with the country's underlying problems, particularly in the economy, with the result that when the moment of reckoning arrived in the 1970s and 1980s it proved all the more acute and painful. The overmanned and under-funded state of the British industrial base which awaited its inevitable fate in the crises of these years stands as the most poignant illustration. In short, the consensus may not simply have coincided with a period of relative decline; it may have helped cause it.

It is largely the political standpoint of the contemporary observer which determines the interpretation he gives to the years of consensus. For the New Right of the 1970s and 1980s the consensus marked the period in which the Conservative Party meekly acquiesced in the drift towards an ever more collectivist and socialistic state, while participating in a conspiracy of rising inflation. For the Bennite or 'hard' left of the Labour Party the consensus involved the abandonment of genuinely socialist goals and a too ready acceptance of a fundamentally capitalist society. By contrast, and while Labour and Conservatives increasingly abandoned the centre ground in the course of the 1970s, others came to regard the postwar years with an affectionate nostalgia. Implicit in the late Lord Stockton's criticisms of Mrs Thatcher's government was the presumption that the country's performance had deteriorated since the time he was Prime Minister. Thus both supporters and detractors of the present government have had good reason to exaggerate the extent to which 1979 marks a break with the past. Their analyses tend to make the ending of the consensus more clear-cut and complete than was perhaps the case.

The most objective assessment perhaps tackles the question in a rather different way. It was in all probability inevitable that something like the postwar consensus would emerge. The generation which had grown up in the depression years of the 1930s, fought the war and experienced the continuing privations which this entailed, demanded that politicians should focus their attention just as soon as it was possible on the creation of a better world. Those who, with the inestimable benefits of hindsight, look back on the supposed missed opportunities of the 1950s and 1960s fail to take note of what was politically possible within a democracy, particularly one which was anxious to enjoy the supposed fruits of the military victory achieved at such great cost. 'There is no alternative' is a political phrase closely associated with the policies and convictions of Margaret Thatcher. Perhaps, however, it was equally appropriate to the years of consensus after 1945.

Bibliography and References

Addison, Paul 1975: *The Road to 1945: British Politics and the Second World War*. London: Cape.

Addison, Paul 1985: *Now the War is Over*. London: Cape.

Attlee, Clement 1954: *As it Happened*. London: Heinemann.

Barnett, Correlli 1986: *The Audit of War*. London: Macmillan.

Barnett, Joel 1982: *Inside the Treasury*. London: Deutsch.

Beer, Samuel 1965: *Modern British Politics*. London: Faber.

Benn, Tony 1988: *Office Without Power. Diaries 1968–72*. London: Hutchinson.

Brittan, Samuel 1964: *The Treasury under the Tories, 1951–1964*. Harmondsworth: Penguin.

Brittan, Samuel 1971: *Steering the Economy*. New York: The Library Press.

Bullock, Alan 1983: *Ernest Bevin: Foreign Secretary 1945–1951*. London: Heinemann.

Burridge, Trevor 1985: *Clement Attlee*. London: Cape.

Butler, David 1989: *British General Elections since 1945*. Oxford: Basil Blackwell.

Butler, R. A. [Lord] 1971: *The Art of the Possible*. London: Hamilton.

Byrnes, James 1947: *Speaking Frankly*. London: Heinemann.

Campbell, John 1987: *Nye Bevan and the Mirage of British Socialism*. London: Weidenfeld & Nicolson.

Castle, Barbara 1980: *The Castle Diaries 1974–76*. London: Weidenfeld & Nicolson.

Castle, Barbara 1984: *The Castle Diaries 1964—70*. London: Weidenfeld & Nicolson.

Childs, David 1986: *Britain Since 1945: A Political History*. London: Benn.

Coates, David 1980: *Labour in Power? A Study of the Labour Government 1974—1979*. London: Longman.

Crossman, Richard 1981: *The Backbench Diaries of Richard Crossman*. ed. Janet Morgan. London: Hamilton.

Duff, Peggy 1971: *Left, Left, Left: A Personal Account of Six Protest Campaigns, 1945—65*. London: Allison & Busby.

Dutton, David 1985: *Austen Chamberlain: Gentleman in Politics*. Bolton: Ross Anderson.

Eatwell, Roger 1979: *The 1945—1951 Labour Governments*. London: Batsford.

Eden, Sir Anthony 1960: *Full Circle*. London: Cassell.

Fisher, Nigel 1973: *Iain Macleod*. London: Deutsch.

Gough, I. 1979: *The Political Economy of the Welfare State*. London: Macmillan.

Gowing, Margaret 1974: *Independence and Deterrence: Britain and Atomic Energy 1945—1952*, vol. I. London: Macmillan.

Hailsham, Lord 1959: *The Conservative Case*. Harmondsworth: Penguin.

Harris, Kenneth 1982: *Attlee*. London: Weidenfeld & Nicolson.

Hennessy, Peter and Seldon, Anthony (eds) 1987: *Ruling Performance: British Governments from Attlee to Thatcher*. Oxford: Basil Blackwell.

Holmes, Martin 1985a: *The Labour Government, 1974—79: Political Aims and Economic Reality*. London: Macmillan.

Holmes, Martin 1985b: *The First Thatcher Government, 1979—83: Contemporary Conservatism and Economic Change*. Brighton: Wheatsheaf.

Horne, Alistair 1988: *Macmillan 1894—1956*. London: Macmillan.

Horne, Alistair 1989: *Macmillan 1957—1986*. London: Macmillan.

Howard, Anthony 1987: *RAB: The Life of R. A. Butler*. London: Cape.

James, Robert Rhodes 1972: *Ambitions and Realities: British Politics 1964—70*. London: Weidenfeld & Nicolson.

James, Robert Rhodes 1986: *Anthony Eden*. London: Weidenfeld & Nicolson.

Jeffreys, Kevin (ed.) 1987a: *Labour and the Wartime Coalition: From the Diary of James Chuter Ede 1941—1945*. London: Historians Press.

Jeffreys, Kevin 1987b: British politics and social policy during the Second World War. *Historical Journal*, 30, pp. 123–44.

Jenkins, Peter 1987: *Mrs. Thatcher's Revolution: the Ending of the Socialist Era*. London: Cape.

Jones, Tudor 1989: Is Labour abandoning its socialist roots? *Contemporary Record*, 3, pp. 6–8.

Joseph, Sir Keith 1987: Escaping the chrysalis of statism. *Contemporary Record*, 1, pp. 26–31.

Kavanagh, Dennis 1987: *Thatcherism and British Politics: The End of Consensus?* Oxford: Oxford University Press.

Kavanagh, Dennis and Morris, Peter 1989: *Consensus Politics from Attlee to Thatcher*. Oxford: Basil Blackwell.

Kellner, Peter 1989: Adapting to the postwar consensus. *Contemporary Record*, 3, pp. 11–15.

Lamb, Richard 1987: *The Failure of the Eden Government*. London: Sidgwick & Jackson.

Lindsay, T. F. and Harrington, Michael 1979: *The Conservative Party 1918–1979*. London: Macmillan.

Macmillan, Harold 1971: *Riding the Storm 1956–1959*. London: Macmillan.

Marquand, David 1988: *The Unprincipled Society*. London: Cape.

Middlemas, Keith 1979: *Politics in Industrial Society: The Experience of the British System Since 1911*. London: Deutsch.

Middlemas, Keith 1986: *Power, Competition and the State: Britain in Search of Balance, 1940–61*. London: Macmillan.

Morgan, Kenneth 1984: *Labour in Power 1945–51*. Oxford: Clarendon Press.

Morgan, Kenneth 1988: Nationalisation and privatisation. *Contemporary Record*, 2, pp. 32–4.

Peden, George 1985: *British Economic and Social Policy: Lloyd George to Margaret Thatcher*. Oxford: Philip Allen.

Peden, George 1988: *Keynes, The Treasury and British Economic Policy*. London: Macmillan.

Pelling, Henry 1984: *The Labour Government 1945–51*. London: Macmillan.

Pimlott, Ben 1985: *Hugh Dalton*. London: Cape.

Pimlott, Ben (ed.) 1986: *The Second World War Diary of Hugh Dalton*. London: Cape/London School of Economics.

Pimlott, Ben 1988: The myth of consensus, in Smith, L. M. (ed.), *The Making of Britain: Echoes of Greatness*. London: Macmillan.

Prior, James 1986: *A Balance of Power*. London: Hamilton.

Ramsden, John 1987: A party for owners or a party for earners. *Transactions of the Royal Historical Society*, 5th series, 37, pp. 49−63.

Riddell, Peter 1983: *The Thatcher Government*. Oxford: Martin Robertson.

Robertson, David 1976: *A Theory of Party Competition*. London: Wiley.

Rose, Richard 1980: *Do Parties Make a Difference?* London: Macmillan.

Seldon, Anthony 1981: *Churchill's Indian Summer: The Conservative Government, 1951−55*. London: Hodder & Stoughton.

Sked, Alan and Cook, Chris 1979: *Post-War Britain: A Political History*. Brighton: Harvester.

Steel, David 1980: *A House Divided: The Lib-Lab Pact and the Future of British Politics*. London: Weidenfeld & Nicolson.

Taylor, Robert 1989: Mrs Thatcher's impact on the TUC. *Contemporary Record*, 2, pp. 23−6.

Thorpe, D. R. 1989: *Selwyn Lloyd*. London: Cape.

Whitehead, Philip 1985: *The Writing on the Wall*. London: Michael Joseph.

Williams, Philip 1979: *Hugh Gaitskell: A Political Biography*. London: Cape.

Wilson, Harold 1979: *Final Term: The Labour Government 1974−1976*. London: Weidenfeld & Nicolson.

Woolton, Lord 1959: *Memoirs*. London: Cassell.

Index

Action not Words, 66
Adam Smith Institute, 82
Addison, Paul, 5, 9; on Labour
 and Conservative Parties, 49;
 on National Health Service,
 30
Agricultural Charter, 38
Agriculture Act (1947), 38
Alexander, A. V., 24
'Alternative Economic Strategy',
 89
Amory, Derick Heathcoat, as
 Chancellor, 53–4
Arab-Israeli War (1973), 69
Assheton, Ralph, 17, 43
Attlee, Clement, 23, 37, 49, 50,
 85, 89; and Labour
 government, 22; and National
 Health Service, 30–1; and
 nationalization, 28; and 1945
 election, 19; and 1951
 election, 39; and 1955
 election, 41; and Potsdam
 Conference, 32; and wartime
 government, 13, 14, 19

balance of payments, 58, 64, 73
Balogh, Thomas, 12

Bank of England, nationalization
 of, 27–8, 38
Barber, Anthony, as Chancellor,
 69, 81
Barnett, Correlli, on wartime
 performance, 11
Beer, Samuel, 37
Benn, Tony, and consensus, 6;
 as Energy Secretary, 73; as
 Industry Secretary, 71; and
 Labour's move to left, 69, 88,
 89; and 1945 government, 22;
 radicalization of, 62; and
 trade unions, 59–60
Berlin blockade, 33–4
Bevan, Aneurin, and consensus,
 88; and Employment White
 Paper, 18; and impact of war,
 10; and National Health
 Service, 29–31; and 1945
 Cabinet, 24
Bevanites, 50
Beveridge, Sir William, 14, 15,
 16, 80, 87
Beveridge Report, 14, 15, 16,
 17, 30
Bevin, Ernest, and centre party,
 42; and Emergency Powers

101

Conservative Research
Department, 37−9
Cripps, Sir Stafford, as
Chancellor, 25, 26
Croham, Lord, 43
Crookshank, Harry, 45
Crosland, Anthony, 50, 70, 88
Crossman, Richard, 43
Czech coup (1948), 33

Dahrendorf, Ralf, 93
Daily Mirror, 40
Dalton, Hugh, 23, 32; on Tory
Reform Committee, 16; as
Chancellor, 25; on Empire,
35
Davies, John, 68
Dawson Report (1920), 30
Deakin, Arthur, 46
defence spending, 35, 52
devaluation, 58
Douglas-Home, Sir Alec, as
Prime Minister, 51, 55, 57,
58, 65, 85

Eatwell, Roger, 6
economic growth, 54, 55, 57, 58,
64, 65, 78
Ede, James Chuter, 17, 24
Eden, Sir Anthony, 13, 28, 32;
and Bevin's foreign policy, 34;
and Europe, 48; as Foreign
Secretary, 47; and 1951
government, 42; as Prime
Minister, 47, 49, 51; and
social reform, 38
Education Act (1944), 17, 20, 31
Educational Reconstruction, 17
electricity, nationalization of, 27
Empire, British, 7, 20, 35, 49
European Defence Community,
48
European integration, 35, 36, 48,
55, 61, 65, 68, 70, 74
Excess Profits Tax, 43

Fair Deal at Work, 59
Feather, Vic, 59
Foot, Michael, 73; as
Employment Secretary, 71; as
Labour leader, 89, 92; and
Miners' Strike, 71−2; and
1951 election, 40
foreign policy: and Eden
government, 52; and 1945
election, 20; and 1945
government, 31−2; and 1951
government, 46−7; and 1964
government, 60−1
Friedman, Milton, 79, 80
full employment, 7, 11, 12, 14,
20, 26, 38, 42, 58, 63, 74, 82;
white paper on, 17
The Future of Socialism, 50
Fyfe, Sir David Maxwell, 36, 43,
48

Gaitskell, Hugh, 2, 22, 43−4,
89; death, 51; as Labour
leader, 50−1; and 1951
budget, 39, 45, 50
gas industry, nationalization of,
27−8; denationalization of,
86
de Gaulle, Charles, 55, 61
General Elections: 1945, 9, 15,
19; 1950, 39, 45; 1951, 4, 5,
45, 51; 1955, 49, 50, 51;
1959, 51, 54; 1964, 56; 1966,
57, 66, 67; 1970, 5, 57, 67;
1974, 71; 1979, 84; 1983, 90;
1987, 92
*General Theory of Employment,
Interest and Money,* 11, 14
Geneva Conference (1954), 47
Gentian Violet, 49
Gowing, Margaret, 34−5
Guillebaud Committee, 45

Hall, George, 36
Harrod, Roy, 53

Hattersley, Roy, 93
von Hayek, Friedrich, 80
Healey, Denis: as Chancellor, 73, 74, 85; and foreign policy, 32; as Labour deputy leader, 89
Heath, Edward: as Conservative leader, 57, 81; and dismissal of Powell, 65; and education, 61; fall of, 69; and move to right, 66; as Prime Minister, 62, 67, 69, 79, 80, 85; and trade unions, 86; and U-turn, 68–9, 82
Heyworth Committee, 28
Hinchingbrooke, Lord, 16
Hogg, Quintin, 92; and social reform, 21; and Tamworth Manifesto, 37, 38; and Tory Reform Committee, 16
Holland, Stuart, and *The Challenge of Socialism*, 70
Holmes, Martin, 83
House of Lords, 90
Howe, Sir Geoffrey, as Chancellor, 83, 84
Hyams, Edward, 49

immigration, 62, 65
In Place of Strife, 59, 67, 71
incomes policy, 67, 72
Indian independence, 35
Industrial Charter, 38
Industrial Relations Act (1971), 68, 70, 71, 86
Industry Bill (1972), 69; (1975), 72
inflation, 12, 26, 53–4, 64, 65, 72, 74, 75, 77, 78, 79, 84, 93, 95
Institute for Economic Affairs, 82
International Monetary Fund, 85

Jay, Peter, 79–80

Jefferys, Kevin, 5, 36–7
Jenkins, Peter, and end of Keynesianism, 88; on Keith Joseph, 81; rejects idea of consensus, 5
Jenkins, Roy: as Chancellor, 58; and Europe, 61; leaves Labour, 89
Jones, Jack, 59, 72
Joseph, Sir Keith, 66; and breakdown of consensus, 63; and free market economics, 81–2, 85; on Heath's government, 66, 80; as Industry Secretary, 83; and new consensus, 92; and ratchet effect, 23, 81

Kavanagh, Dennis, 83
'Keep Left Group', 33
Keynes, John Maynard, 11, 12, 18, 44, 80, 88; and inflation, 63; and 1945 economic situation, 25
Keynesian economics, 12, 16, 17, 26, 42, 44, 51, 53, 63, 65, 73, 74, 75, 79, 83, 85, 93
Kinnock, Neil, 90
Korean War, 34, 44, 52

Labour Believes in Britain, 27
Labour Party, 6, 7, 8; and Beveridge Report, 16; and Coalition government, 13, 14; and Commonwealth, 48; and Conference (1952), 50; decline of, 51–2; drift to left, 69, 88, 95; and Europe, 48, 70, 74, 90, 93; and foreign policy, 60–1; and Liberals, 5, 57; and management of economy, 25; and Marxism, 26; and monetarism, 74; and nationalization, 18, 27, 29; and 1945 election, 20; and

104

Conservative Party and, 77;
excessive power of, 72, 78,
82; Labour Party and, 71, 89;
reform of, 53, 58–60, 62, 66,
67, 68, 86, 93; and war, 13,
41
Trade Union Congress (TUC),
60, 75, 86
Treaty of Rome (1957), 48

unemployment, 16, 53–4, 64,
65, 68, 72, 75, 78, 79, 84, 87
unilateral nuclear disarmament,
51
Upper Clyde Shipbuilders, 69,
85

Vietnam War, 60, 62, 64

Wall, Pat, 89
water, privatization of, 86, 93
welfare state, 7, 25, 37, 39, 41,
45, 82, 85, 87, 94

Whitehead, Philip, 74
Wilkinson, Ellen, 24, 31
Willink, Henry, 30
Wilson, Harold, 80, 89; and
'bonfire of controls', 26, 43;
and Europe, 61; as Labour
leader, 51, 55, 56; and
Labour moderation, 74, 91;
and Mansion House speech,
60; and 1964 election, 56; as
Prime Minister, 58–9, 62,
71; reputation of, 57;
resignation of (1951), 49–50;
and 'Selsdon Man', 67; and
socialism, 56; and steel
industry, 57; and trade
unions, 59–60, 68, 87
winter of discontent, 75
Wood, Sir Kingsley, 15
Woolton, Lord, 45, 46